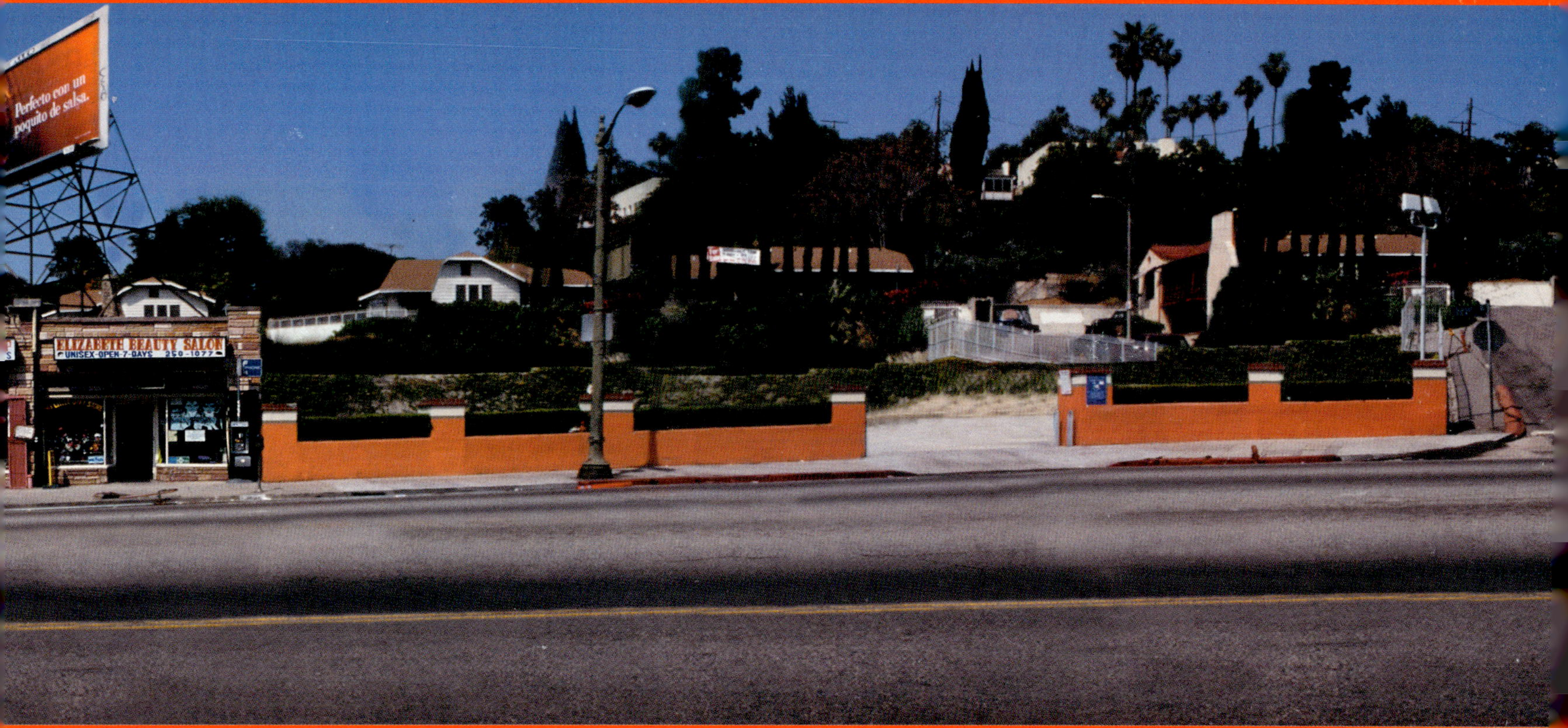

GLEN SEATOR *THREE*

Glen Seator: Three publication © 1999 Gagosian Gallery, Los Angeles
Kinesthetic Capital: Glen Seator's Three © 1999 David Joselit
Glen Seator's Daring Desiring Machines © 1999 Terry R. Myers

Design by Bruce Mau Design Inc., Bruce Mau with Barr Gilmore
Printed by Cantz, Germany on Strobe Dull Coated and f-color sandbeige
Installation photography of *Three* by Douglas M. Parker
Additional photography by Ben Blackwell, Kevin Clarke, Geoffrey Clements, Joseph Coscia, Barr Gilmore, Volker Naumann, Hans Schubert, and Glen Seator
AutoCAD drawings by Bill Mulvey
Edited by Kay Pallister and Glen Seator

Gagosian Gallery Co-ordinators: Pippa Cohen, Kay Pallister, Susan Jensen and Jim Webb
The Gagosian Gallery would like to thank: Vicki Reynolds, Council Member, City of Beverly Hills, Chris Ogata, Mark Nierman, BPPR, Popular Cash Express, Los Angeles, Matthew Hayden Construction, VC Signs, C&H Metal Products, Ocean Glass & Metal Co., Smith Electric, Davis Flourescent, Total Control Plastering, Renteria, Environmental Pacific Services, Custom Panoramic Lab, Muse-X Imaging and Seven. Additional thanks to everyone involved with the catalogue including: Bruce Mau, Barr Gilmore and Amanda Sebris at Bruce Mau Design, Toronto; William Mulvey, Architect, New York; Doug and Fran Parker Photography, Los Angeles and David Joselit and Terry Myers, Los Angeles.
Glen Seator wishes to thank: Larry Gagosian and the Gagosian Gallery staff, Kay Pallister, Robert Shapazian, Bob Monk, Ealan Wingate, Jim Webb, Pippa Cohen, Candy Coleman, Susan Jensen, Lisa Kenney, Alex Heminway and Robert Levine; Bruce Mau, Barr Gilmore and Amanda Sebris for their startling patience through the making of this catalogue; David Joselit, Terry Myers, Doug and Fran Parker for their words and photos; the production team – Bill Mulvey, Charles Sanchez, Joshua White, Paul Ballatine, Mark Segal, Victor Castenada, Matthew and Colin Hayden, Jane Hart, Jim Cherry, Jill Leckner, Peter and Addie Lorber, Primitivo Suarez and Tom Simpson; Julia Bloomfield for sharing her friendship and home; Patricia Marshall whose timely request for a small Coke led us to *one* of our destinations; fellow travelers – Janet C., Michelle K., Bigi, Tamar, Joel S., Haim, Gwen, Freddie, Mickie and Trotsky; and Joel Wachs and Vicki Reynolds for getting us through the initial hurdles. More appreciation to everyone who helped realize past projects, including: Bill Arning, Britt Arbelius, Alanna Heiss, Matt Hausman, Ryszard Wasko, Anda Rottenberg, Connie Butler, Christoph Grünenberg, Sebastian Clough, Burnett Miller, Thomas Kellein, Bruno Bürgin, Christian Schoch, Markus Brüderlin, Sean Casey, Ann Miller, Martin Kunz, Martin Fritz, Guy Nordenson, Lisa Phillips, Lousie Neri, Irene Tsatsos, Steve Oliver, Ann Hatch, Stein Berre, Jay Jopling, Julia Royce, Mark Darbyshire, Scott Pfaffman, Jonathan Viner, Mary Boone, David Hirsh and Carlton Bright; Vera and Joachim Oeri for their kind hospitality; Gabriella, mi primera aficionada en la vida; and Bartek, who reminds me that, wherever you go, there you are.

CONTENTS

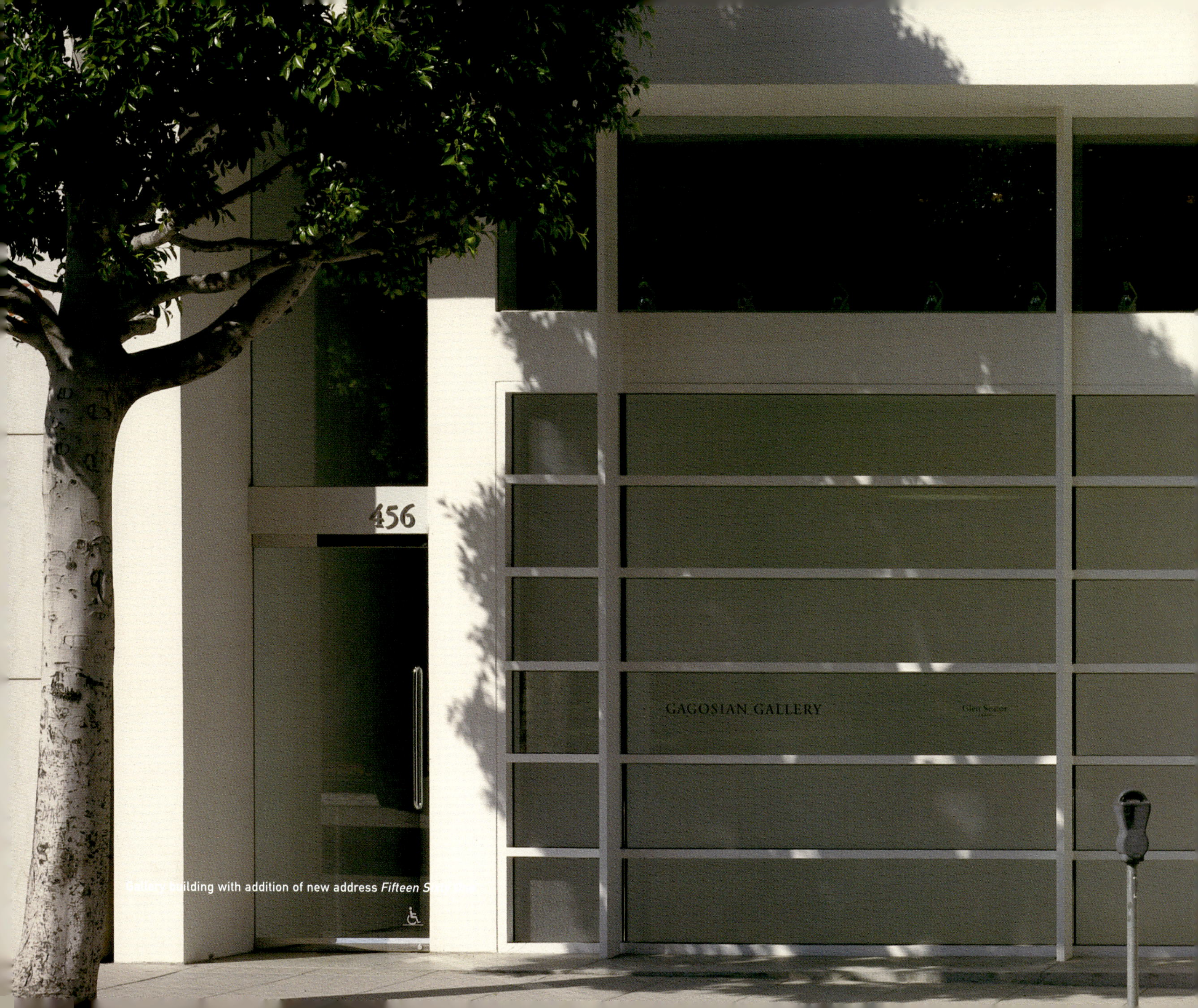

Gallery building with addition of new address *Fifteen S...*

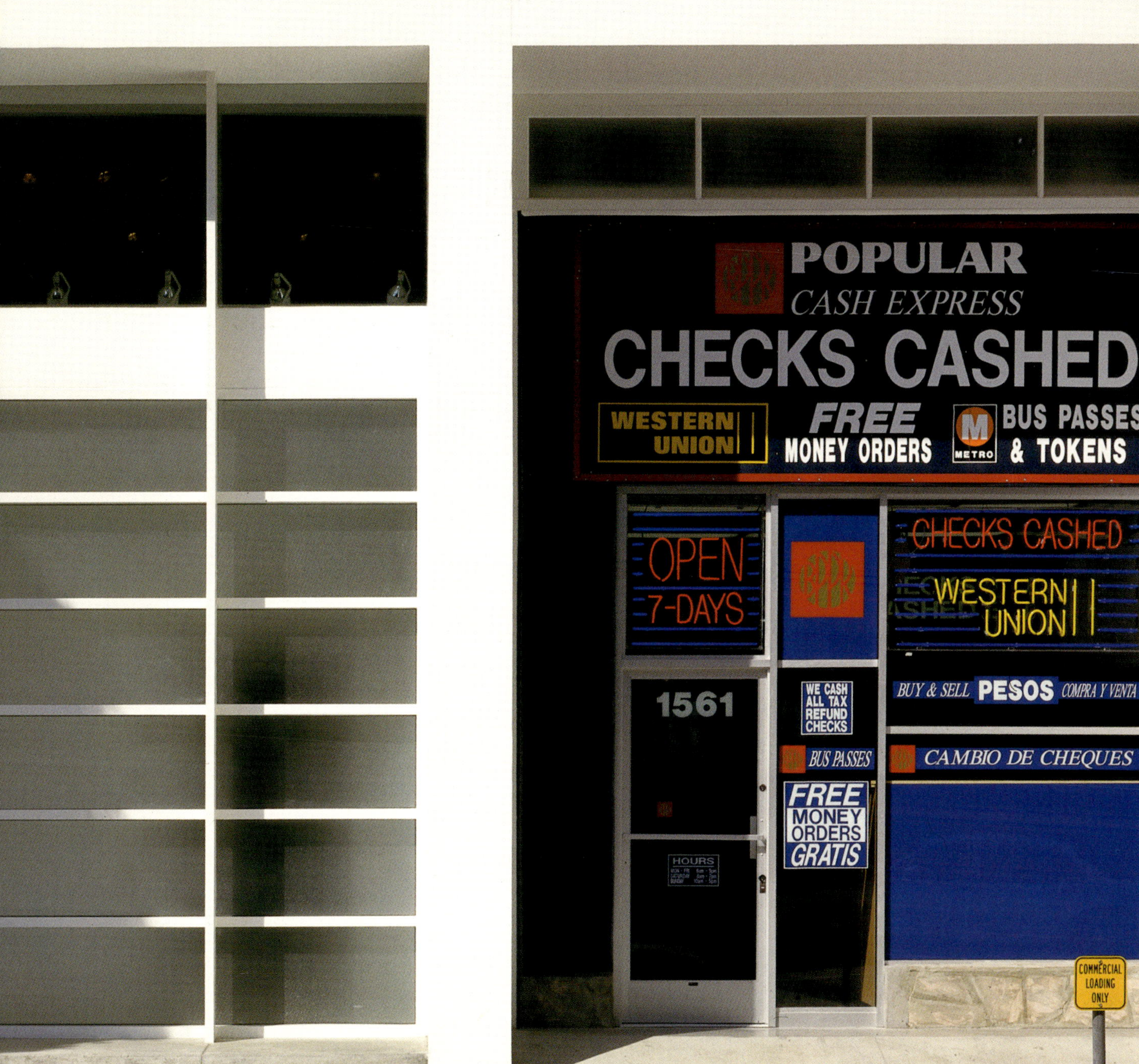
POPULAR
CASH EXPRESS
CHECKS CASHED
WESTERN UNION
FREE
MONEY ORDERS
METRO
BUS PASSES
& TOKENS
OPEN
7-DAYS
CHECKS CASHED
WESTERN UNION
1561
WE CASH
ALL TAX
REFUND
CHECKS
BUY & SELL PESOS COMPRA Y VENTA
BUS PASSES
CAMBIO DE CHEQUES
FREE
MONEY
ORDERS
GRATIS
HOURS
COMMERCIAL
LOADING
ONLY

Popular Cash Express, 1561 Sunset Boulevard, Los Angeles

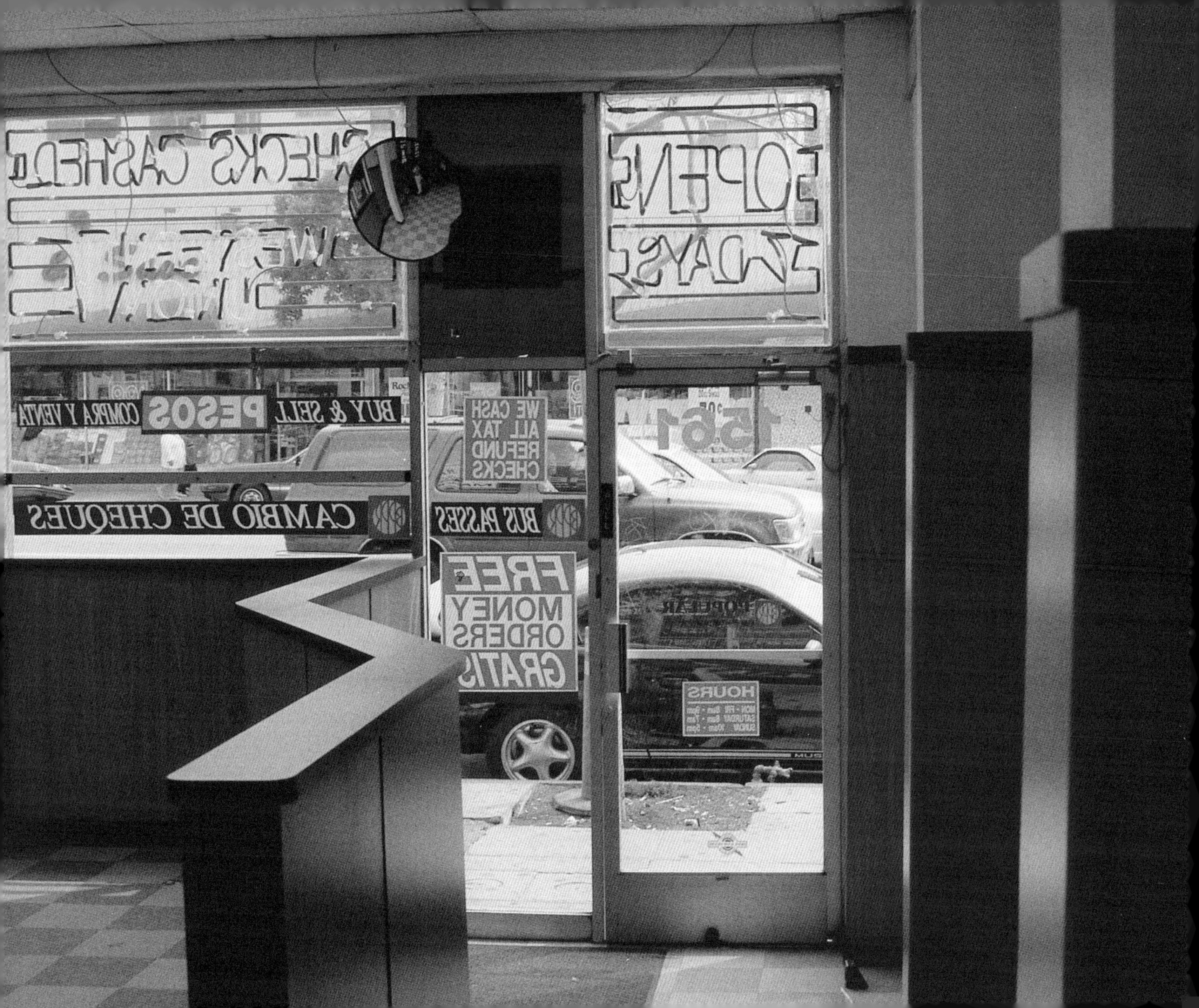

CHECKS CASHED
WE'RE #1
OPENS
7DAYS
PESOS
COMPRA Y VENTA
BUY & SELL
WE CASH
ALL TAX
REFUND
CHECKS
CAMBIO DE CHEQUES
BUS PASSES
FREE
MONEY
ORDERS
GRATIS
POPULAR
1561
HOURS

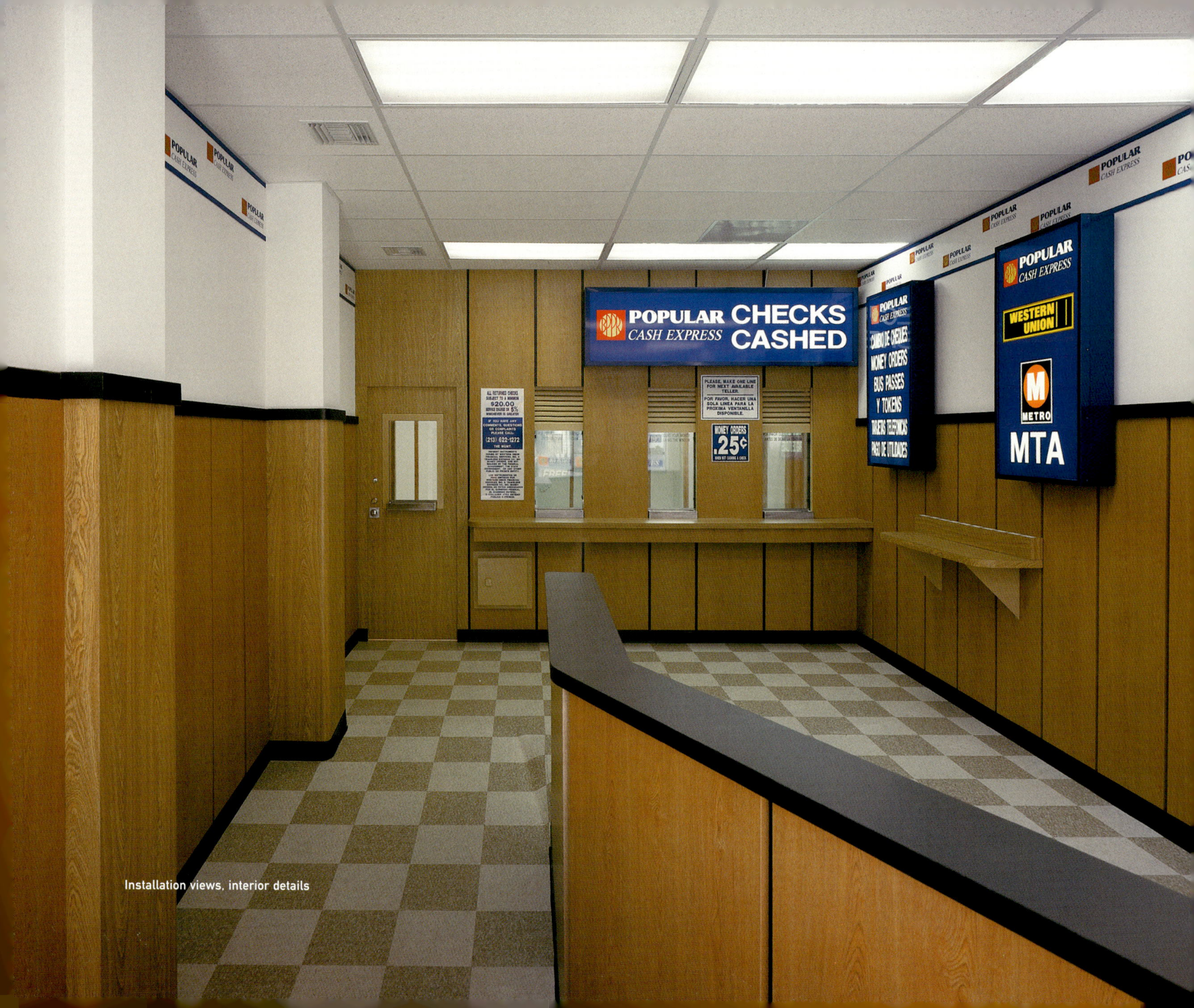

Installation views, interior details

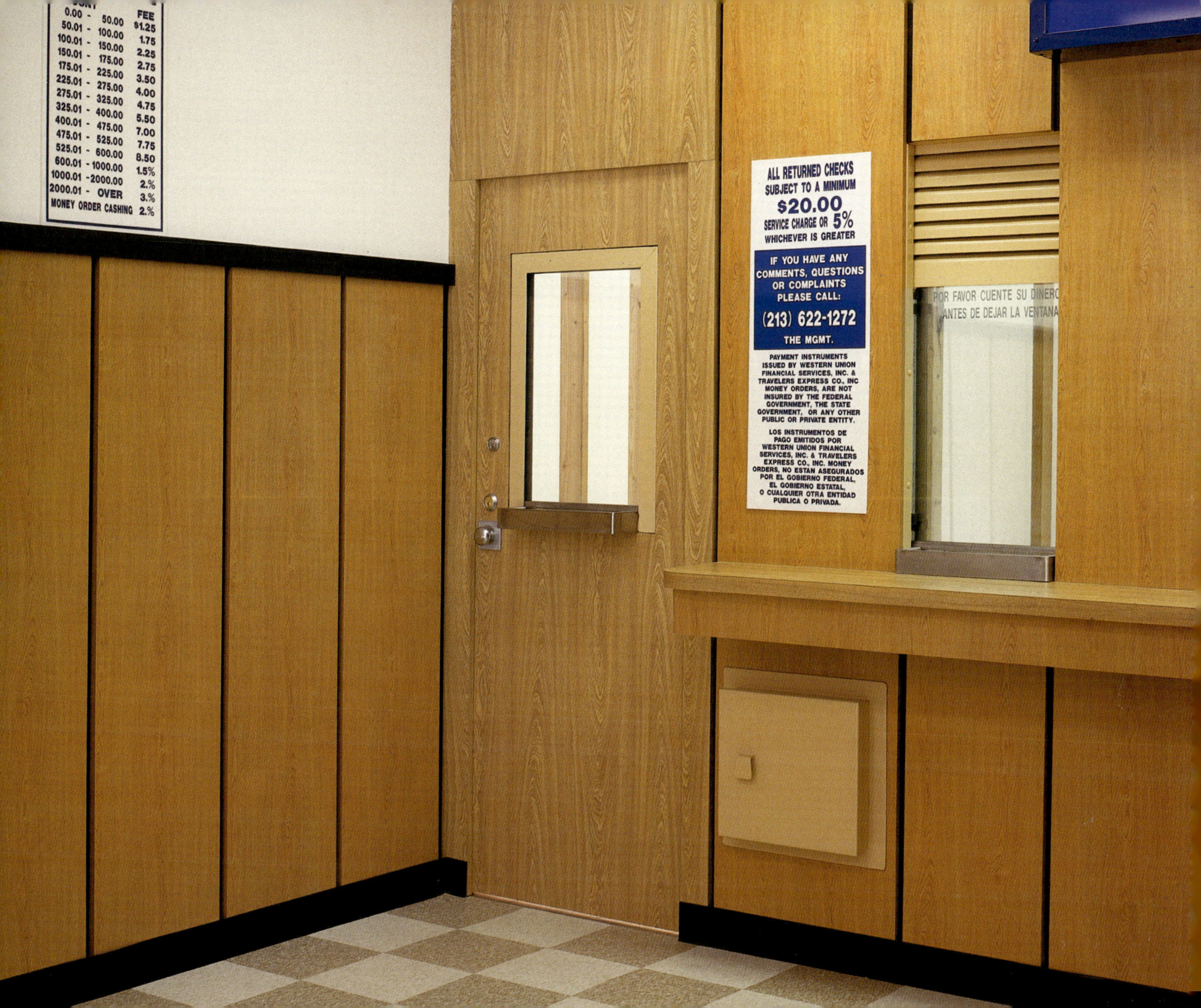
FEE
0.00 - 50.00 $1.25
50.01 - 100.00 1.75
100.01 - 150.00 2.25
150.01 - 175.00 2.75
175.01 - 225.00 3.50
225.01 - 275.00 4.00
275.01 - 325.00 4.75
325.01 - 400.00 5.50
400.01 - 475.00 7.00
475.01 - 525.00 7.75
525.01 - 600.00 8.50
600.01 - 1000.00 1.5%
1000.01 - 2000.00 2.%
2000.01 - OVER 3.%
MONEY ORDER CASHING 2.%
ALL RETURNED CHECKS
SUBJECT TO A MINIMUM
$20.00
SERVICE CHARGE OR 5%
WHICHEVER IS GREATER
IF YOU HAVE ANY
COMMENTS, QUESTIONS
OR COMPLAINTS
PLEASE CALL:
(213) 622-1272
THE MGMT.
PAYMENT INSTRUMENTS
ISSUED BY WESTERN UNION
FINANCIAL SERVICES, INC. &
TRAVELERS EXPRESS CO, INC
MONEY ORDERS, ARE NOT
INSURED BY THE FEDERAL
GOVERNMENT, THE STATE
GOVERNMENT, OR ANY OTHER
PUBLIC OR PRIVATE ENTITY.
LOS INSTRUMENTOS DE
PAGO EMITIDOS POR
WESTERN UNION FINANCIAL
SERVICES, INC. & TRAVELERS
EXPRESS CO., INC. MONEY
ORDERS, NO ESTAN ASEGURADOS
POR EL GOBIERNO FEDERAL,
EL GOBIERNO ESTATAL,
O CUALQUIER OTRA ENTIDAD
PUBLICA O PRIVADA.
POR FAVOR CUENTE SU DINERO
ANTES DE DEJAR LA VENTANA

City of Beverly Hills
Beverly Hills Municipal Code
September 1988

Article 30. Architectural Commission, Architectural Review, and Procedure

Sec. 10-3.3001. Architectural review.

The Council hereby finds that Beverly Hills is internationally known and has become a worldwide synonym for beauty, quality, and value; that by far the largest area of the community is zoned for single-family residences, but a significant part is zoned for apartment, commercial, and industrial uses; that most persons who travel through Beverly Hills or do business in and with Beverly Hills do so in its apartment, commercial, and industrial areas; that there is a tendency of some owners and developers in these areas to disregard beauty and quality in construction and consequent serious danger that construction of inferior quality and appearance in the apartment, commercial, and industrial areas will degrade and depreciate the image, beauty, and reputation of Beverly Hills with adverse consequences for the entire City, including single-family residential areas as well as apartment, commercial, and industrial areas; and that poor quality of design in the exterior appearance of buildings erected in any neighborhood or in the development and maintenance of structures, landscaping, signs, and general appearances affect the desirability of the immediate area and neighboring areas for residential and business purposes or other uses and, by so doing, impair the benefits of occupancy of existing property in such areas, impair the stability in value of both improved and unimproved real property in such areas, prevent the most appropriate development of such areas, produce undesirable conditions affecting the health, safety, comfort, and general welfare of the inhabitants of the City, and destroy the proper relationship between the taxable value of real property in such areas and the cost of municipal services provided therefor. It is the purpose of this Article to prevent these and other harmful effects of such exterior appearances of buildings erected in any neighborhood and thus to promote and protect the health, safety, comfort, and general welfare of the community, to promote the public convenience and prosperity, to conserve the value of buildings, and to encourage the most appropriate use of land within the City.

Sec. 10-3.3002. Architectural Commission.

An Architectural Commission is hereby established which shall consist of seven (7) members who shall be appointed by the Council. At least one (1) of the members shall be appointed from each of the following desciplines: building construction, architecture, landscape architecture, and visual and graphic design, and at least three (3) members shall be laypersons. In the event no person is eligible for appointment in the designated field who is a resident of the City, the Council may waive the residency requirement.

Sec. 10.3.3007. Architectural review required.

(a) (1) No building, structure, sign, wall, fence, or landscaping located in any zone other than a single-family (one-family) residential zone shall be erected, constructed, altered, or remodeled unless the elevations and plans for the exterior portions and areas and the interiors of mall areas, as defined in Section 10-3.147 of Article 1 of this Chapter, Have first been reviewed and approved by the Architectural Commission, or by the Council on appeal.

(2) Exception. Notwithstanding the provisions of subsection (a) (1) of this Section 10-3.3007, temporary seasonal decorations may be displayed on private property, without architectural review, during the period between November 15th of each year and January 10th of the following year.

(b) No exterior portion or area of an existing building, structure, sign, wall, fence, or other improvement to real property, or the interior of any mall area, located in any zone other than a residential zone shall be painted, repainted, textured, or retextured unless the plans, colors, and textures for such work have been reviewed and approved by the Architectural Commission, or by the Council on appeal.

(c) No permit shall be issued for any work described in subsections (a) and (b) of this section and unless the necessary approval required therefor is first granted.

Prior to the commencement of any work described in subsections (a) and (b) of this section, an application for approval shall be made in writing to the Architectural Commission pursuant to the procedure set forth in this Article.

(d) Notwithstanding Open Air Dining Plan approval pursuant to Title 10, Chapter 3, Article 35 of this Code, no open air dining operations shall be established unless the plans for all improvements, fixtures, structures and facilities to be located in the public right of way have been reviewed and approved by the Architectural Commission, or by the Council on appeal. For the purpose of this subsection "facilities" shall include, but not be limited to, tables and chairs.

(e) When, in the opinion of the City Planning Official, the approval of an application for a minor or insignificant permit does not defeat the purposes and objectives of this Article, the Official may grant the approval without submitting the matter to the Architectural Commission for its approval, notwithstanding any other provision of this Section or this Article. The decision of the City Planning Official may be appealed to the Architectural Commission by filing an appeal petition with the City Planning Official no later than fourteen days after the Official's decision. The petition shall be on a form designated by the City Planning Official.

An application which involves the display of any neon element on the exterior of a building, or any neon element in the interior of a building which is displayed in such a manner to make such element visible from a public street or alley, shall not be a minor or insignificant permit within the meaning of this subsection.

(f) Notwithstanding the provisions of this Section, architectural review may be a condition of the granting of a conditional use permit or a variance when required for any use or improvement in a residential zone.

(g) Notwithstanding any other provision of the Section, architectural review shall be a condition of the grant of a sign accomodation pursuant to Article 9 of Chapter 4 of this Title 10.

Sec. 10-3.3008. Building relocation.

The Architectural Commission shall review all plans submitted with applications for moving buildings within or into the City. Photographs shall be included with the application showing all elevations, the structure proposed to be moved, the proposed site, and the buildings adjacent to the proposed site. The Commission shall determine whether the building proposed to be moved will fit harmoniously into the neighborhood wherein it is to be located. The Commission may approve, approve with conditions, or disapprove the issuance of a permit to move such building.

Sec. 10-3.3009. Procedure.

(a) Preliminary sketches of the design of a proposed structure or alteration may be submitted to the Planning Department for informal review so that an applicant may be informed of Architectural Commission policies prior to preparing working drawings. If approved, such sketches shall serve as a guide in the further consideration of the same proposed building or structure.

The applicant for a building permit, when subject to the requirements of this Article, shall submit to the Director of Planning a site plan, as defined by Section 10-3.3012 of this Article, and exterior elevations and such other data as will assist the Architectural Commission and the Director of Planning in evaluating the proposed building or structure.

Final plans and elevations shall be drawn to scale upon substantial paper or cloth and shall be of sufficient clarity to indicate the nature and extent of the work proposed and show in detail that it will conform to the provisions of this Code. The first sheet of each set of plans shall give the street address of the work and the name and address of the owner and the person who prepared the plans. The final plot plan shall conform to Section 10-3.3012 of this Article. Work not thus presented may be rejected by the Director of Planning.

(b) The Director of Planning shall refer such plans to the Architectural Commission at its next regular meeting. If such meeting is not scheduled within the period set for Architectural Commission action, a special meeting shall be called. The Architectural Commission shall act on the application within thirty (30) days after the filing of full and complete data, unless an extension of time is consented to by the applicant.

Sec. 10-3.3010. Criteria.

The Architectural Commission may approve, approve with conditions, or disapprove the issuance of a building permit in any matter subject to its jurisdiction after consideration of whether the following criteria are complied with:

(a) The plan for the proposed building or structure is in conformity with good taste and good design and, in general, contributes to the image of Beverly Hills as a place of beauty, spaciousness, balance, taste, fitness, broad vistas, and high quality;

(b) The plan for the proposed building or structure indicates the manner in which the structure is reasonably protected against external and internal noise, vibrations, and other factors which may tend to make the environment less desirable;

(c) The proposed building or structure is not, in its exterior design and appearance, of inferior quality such as to cause the nature of the local environment to materially depreciate in appearance and value;

(d) The proposed building or structure is in harmony with the proposed developments on land in the general area, with the General Plan for Beverly Hills, and with any precise plans adopted pursuant to the General Plan; and

(e) The proposed development is in conformity with the standards of this Code and other applicable laws insofar as the location and appearance of the buildings and structures are involved.

If the criteria set forth in this Section are met, the application shall be approved. Conditions may be applied when the proposed building or structure does not comply with such criteria and shall be such as to bring such building or structure into conformity. If an application is disapproved, the Architectural Commission shall detail in its findings the criterion or criteria that are not met. The action taken by the Architectural Commission shall be reduced to writing and signed by the chairman, and a copy thereof shall be made available to the applicant upon request.

A decision or order of the Architectural Commission or the Director of Planning shall not become effective until the expiration of fourteen (14) calendar days after the date upon which a ruling of the Architectural Commission or the Director of Planning has been made.

Sec. 10-3.3012. Site plans.

A site plan shall be drawn to scale and shall indicate the following sufficiently for the consideration of visual, safety, and economic factors:

(a) The dimensions and orientation of the parcel;

(b) The location of the buildings and structures, both existing and proposed;

(c) The location of off-street parking and loading facilities;

(d) The location and dimensions of present and proposed street and highway dedications required to handle the traffic generated by the proposed uses;

(e) The location of the points of entry and exit for motor vehicles and the internal circulation pattern;

(f) The location of walls and fences and the indication of their height and the materials of their construction;

(g) An indication of the exterior lighting standards and devices adequate to review the possible hazards and disturbances to the public and adjacent properties;

(h) The location and size of the exterior signs and outdoor advertising;

(i) A preliminary landscaping plan;

(j) The grading and slopes where they affect the relationship of the buildings;

(k) An indication of the heights of buildings and structures;

(l) An indication of the proposed use of the buildings shown on the site; and

(m) Such other architectural and engineering data as may be required to permit the necessary findings that the provisions of this Code are being complied with.

The requirements set forth in subsections (a) through (m) of this Section may be waived by the Director of Planning if he deems the information not essential.

Where an attachment or minor addition to an existing building or structure is proposed, the site plan shall indicate the relationship of such proposal to the existing development.

Sec. 10-3.3013. Encroachments.

Applications for permission to encroach upon City property, such as refacing a building, may be referred to the Architectural Commission. The Commission shall make recommendations to the Council in such cases as to whether the alterations proposed would conform to the standards set forth in this Article.

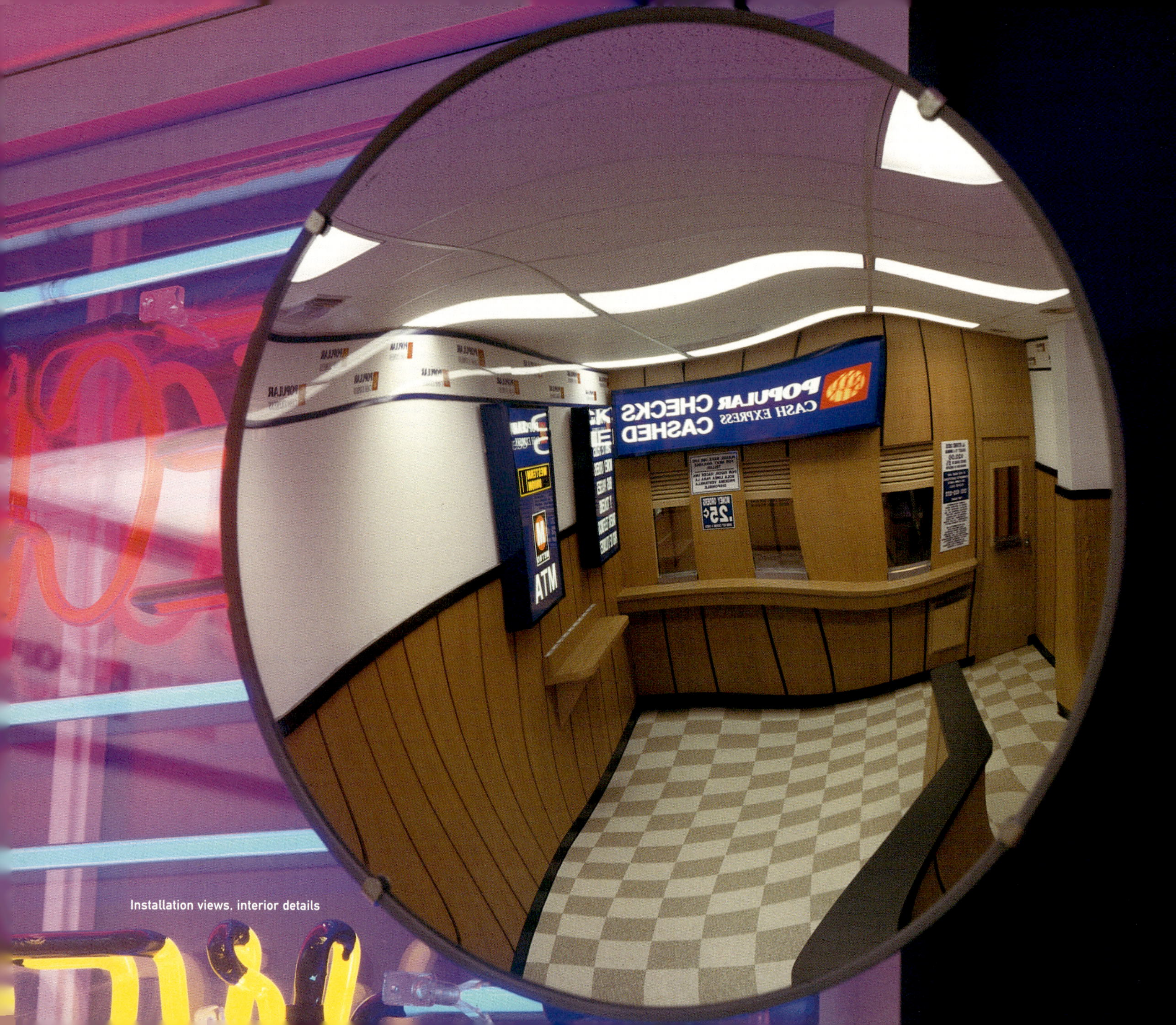

Installation views, interior details

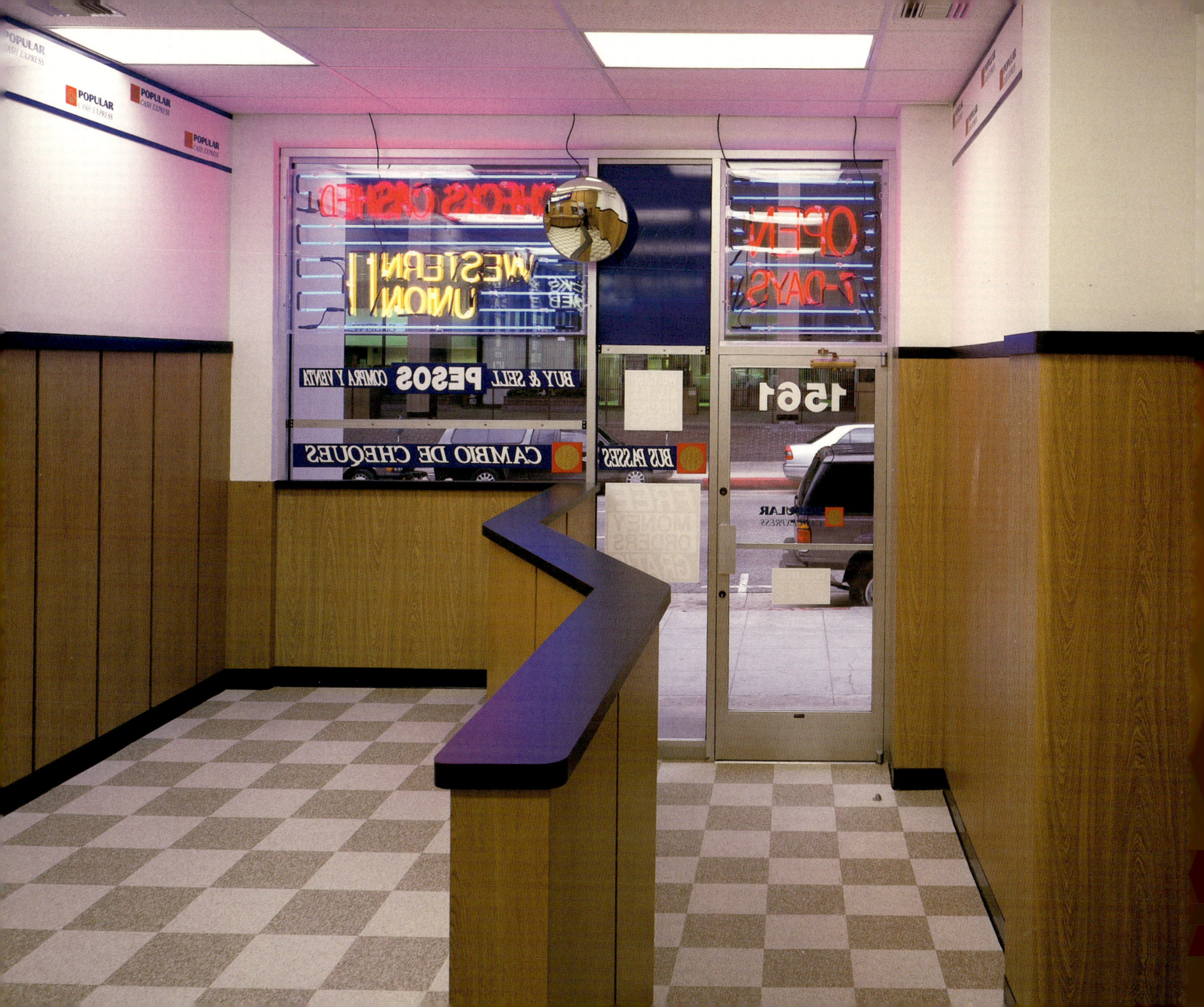
POPULAR
CASH EXPRESS
WESTERN UNION
OPEN 7 DAYS
PESOS BUY & SELL COMPRA Y VENTA
CAMBIO DE CHEQUES
1561
FREE MONEY ORDERS
POPULAR CASH EXPRESS

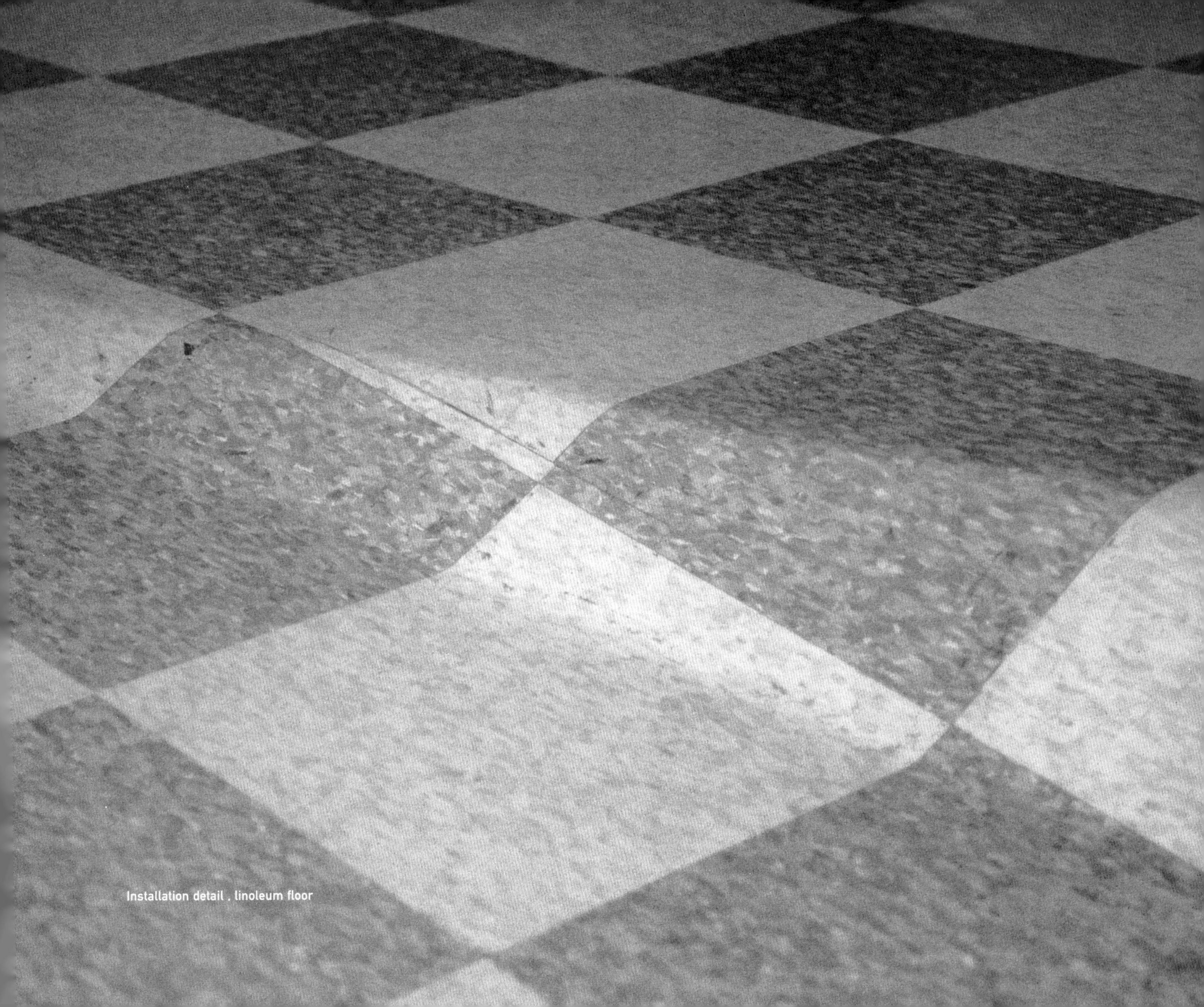

Installation detail . linoleum floor

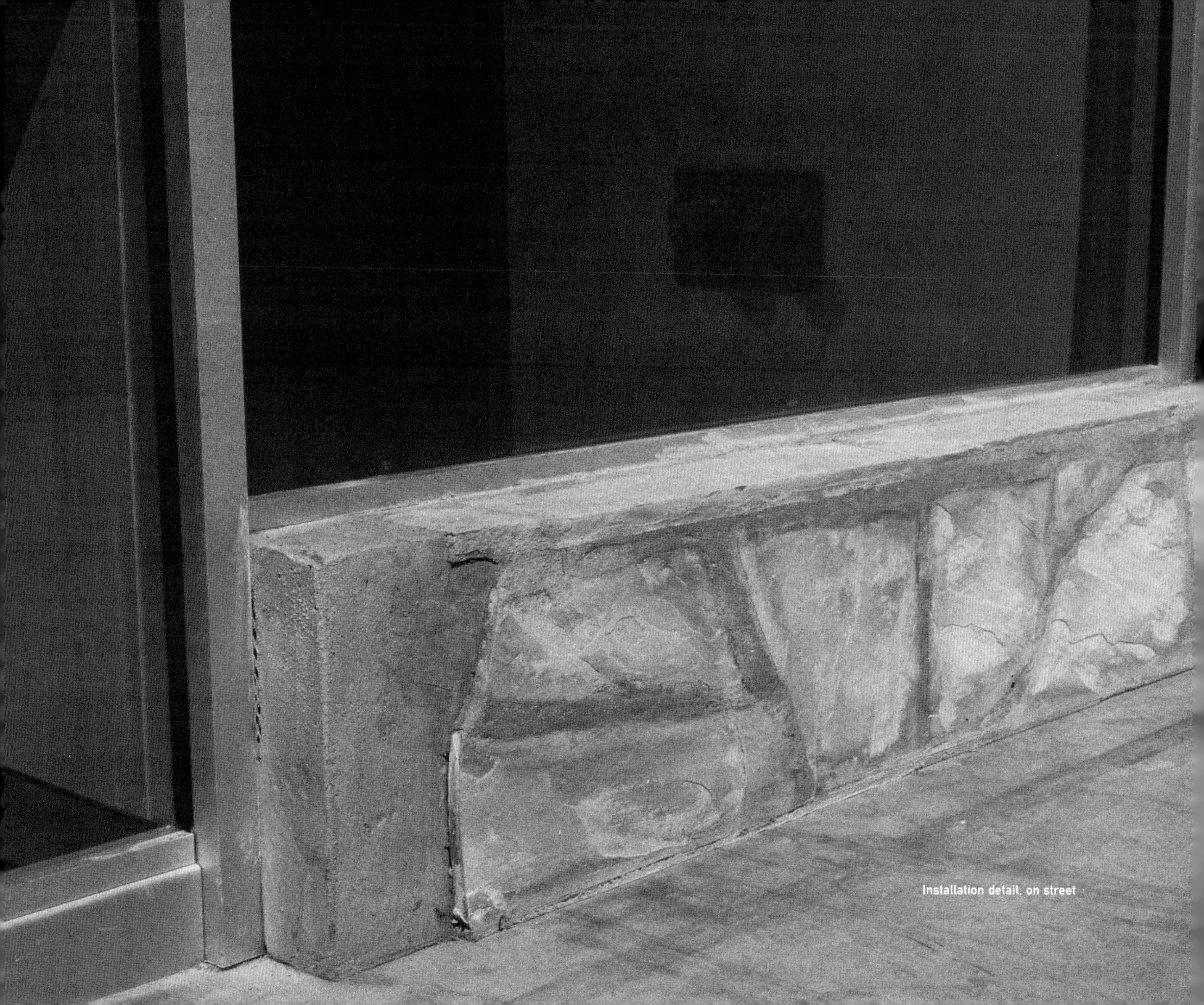
Installation detail, on street

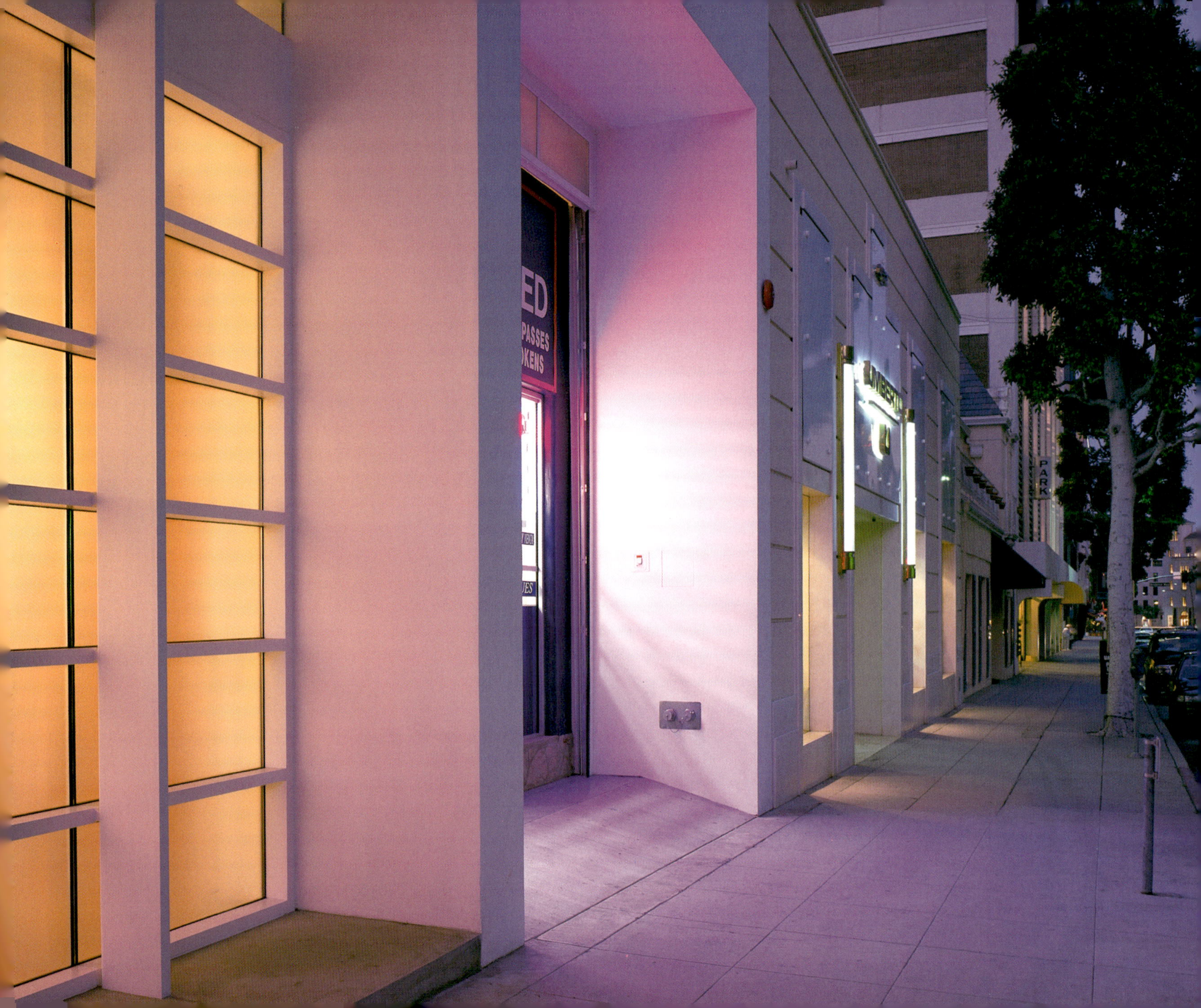
ED
PASSES
KENS
PARK

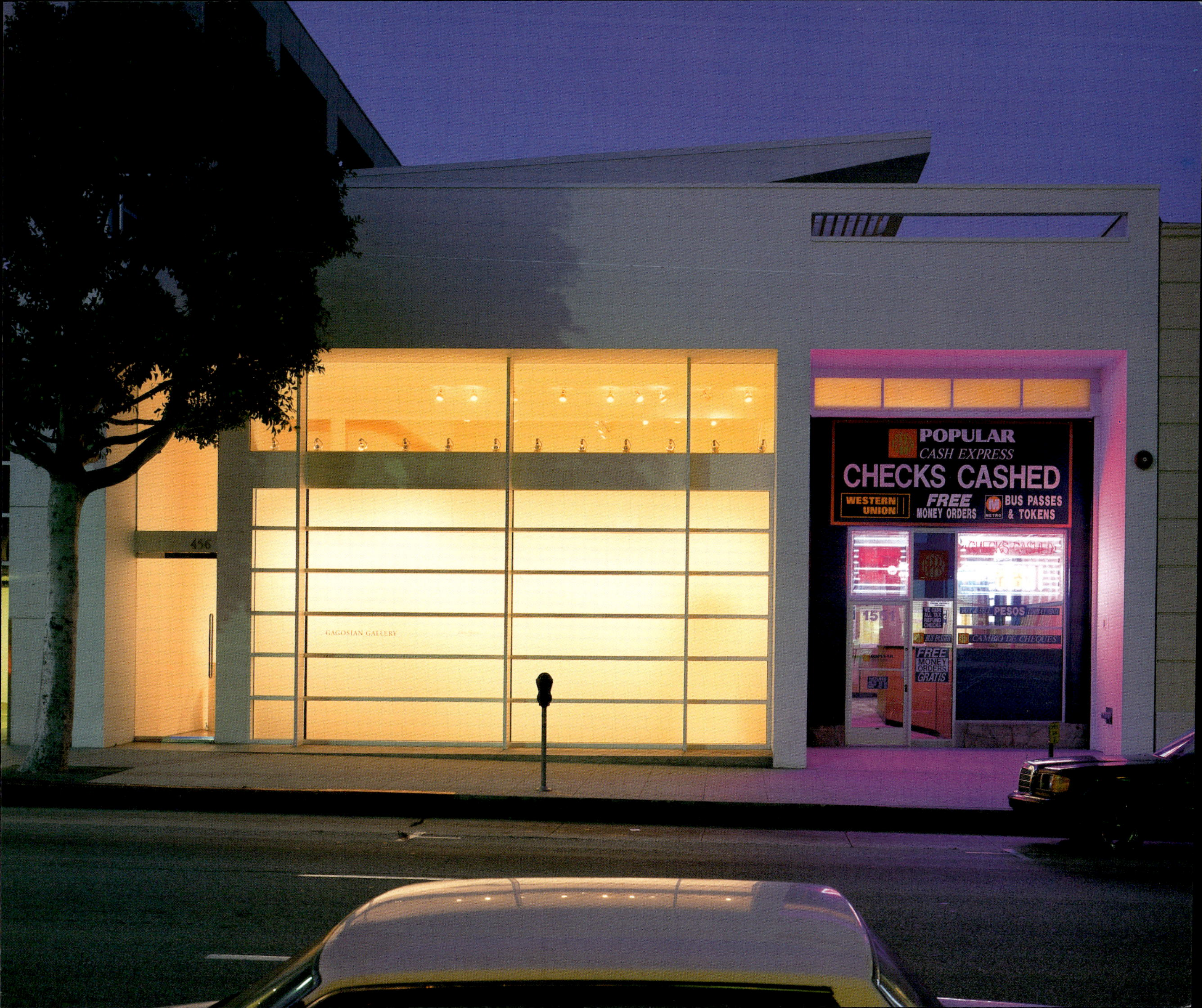
456
GAGOSIAN GALLERY
POPULAR
CASH EXPRESS
CHECKS CASHED
WESTERN UNION
FREE MONEY ORDERS
METRO BUS PASSES & TOKENS
PESOS
CAMBIO DE CHEQUES
FREE MONEY ORDERS GRATIS

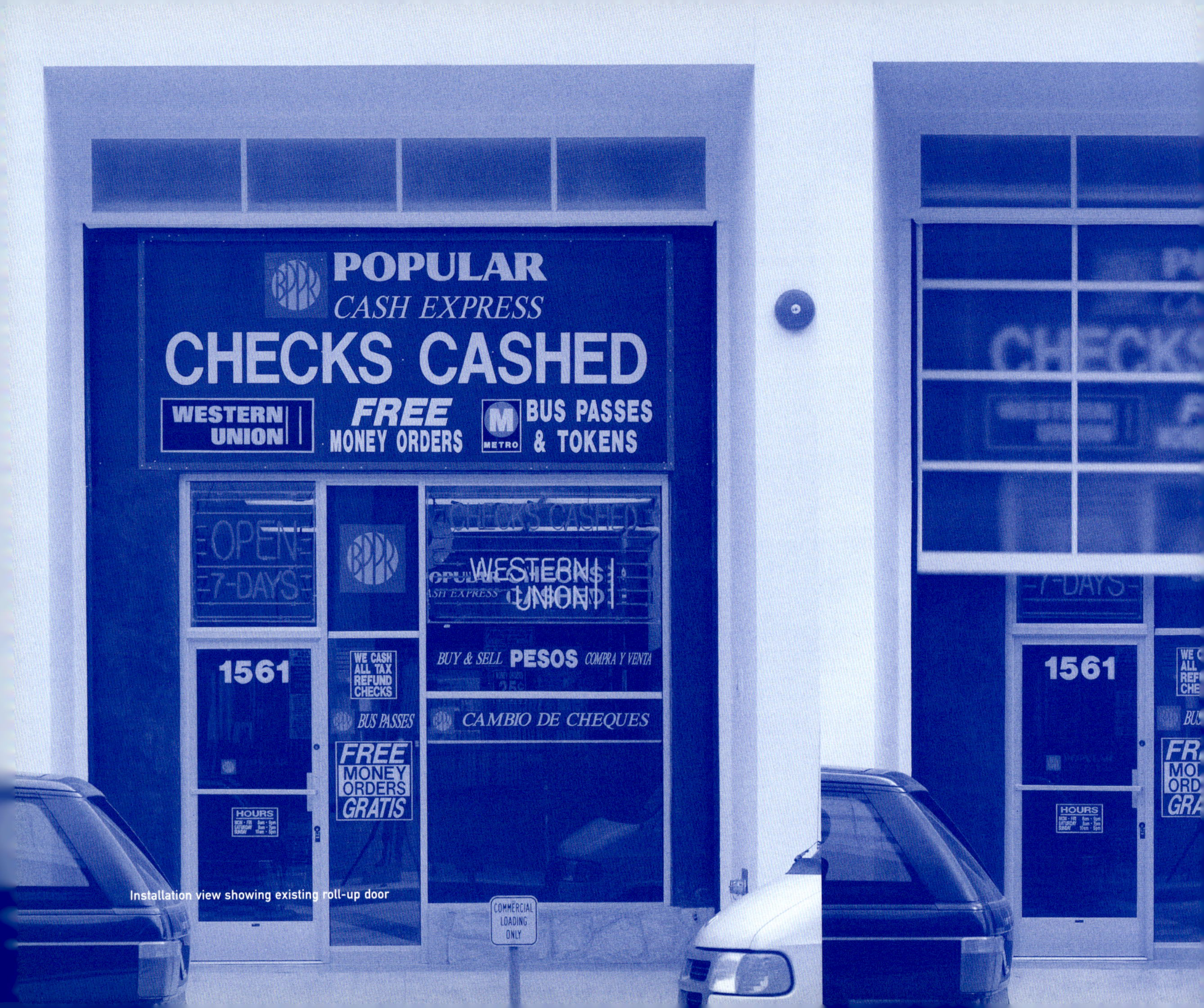

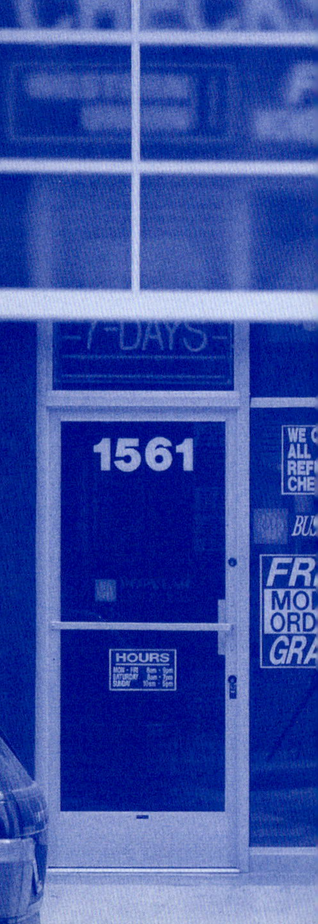

Installation view showing existing roll-up door

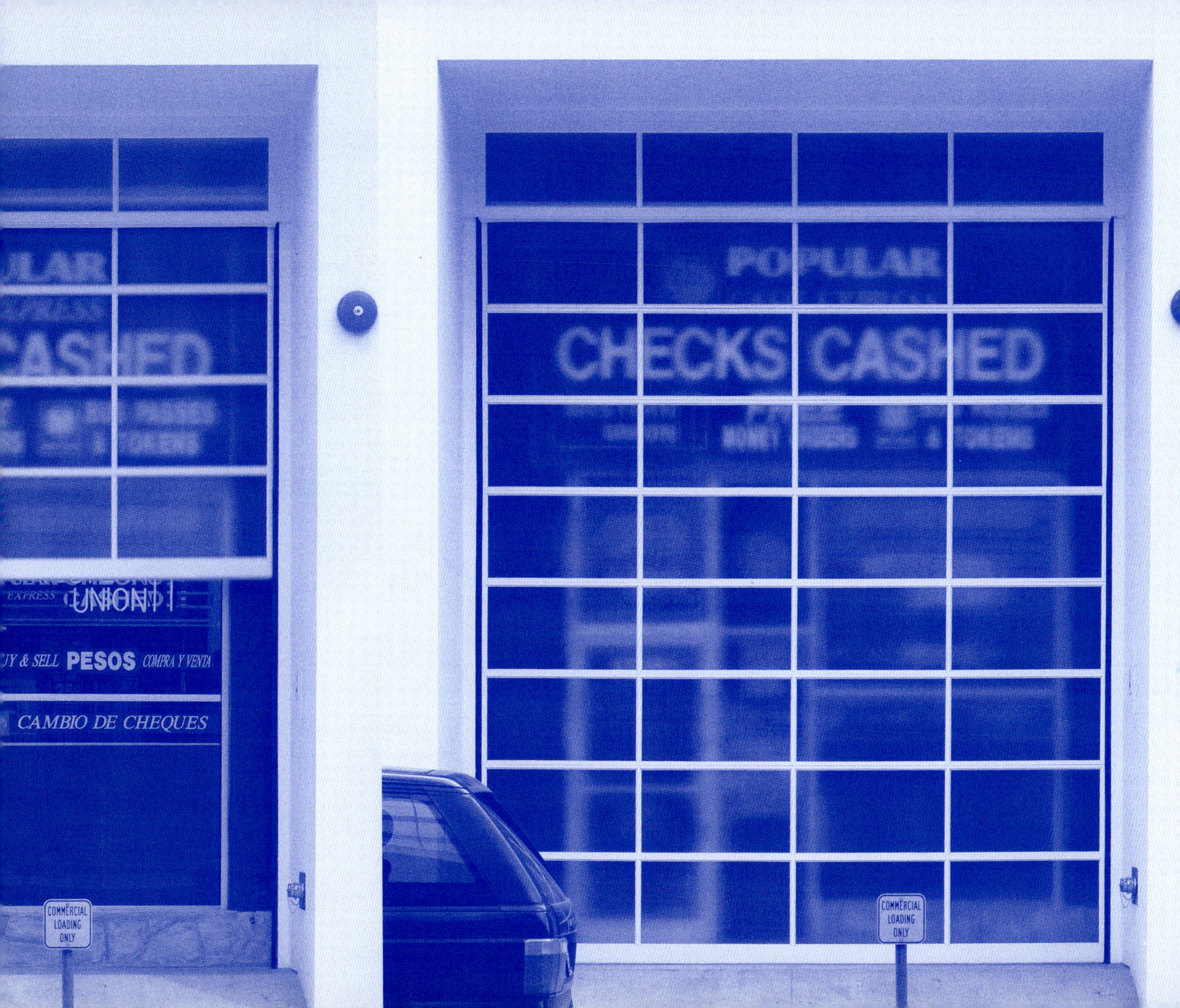
POPULAR
CHECKS CASHED
UNION
EXPRESS
BUY & SELL PESOS COMPRA Y VENTA
CAMBIO DE CHEQUES
CASHED
COMMERCIAL LOADING ONLY
COMMERCIAL LOADING ONLY

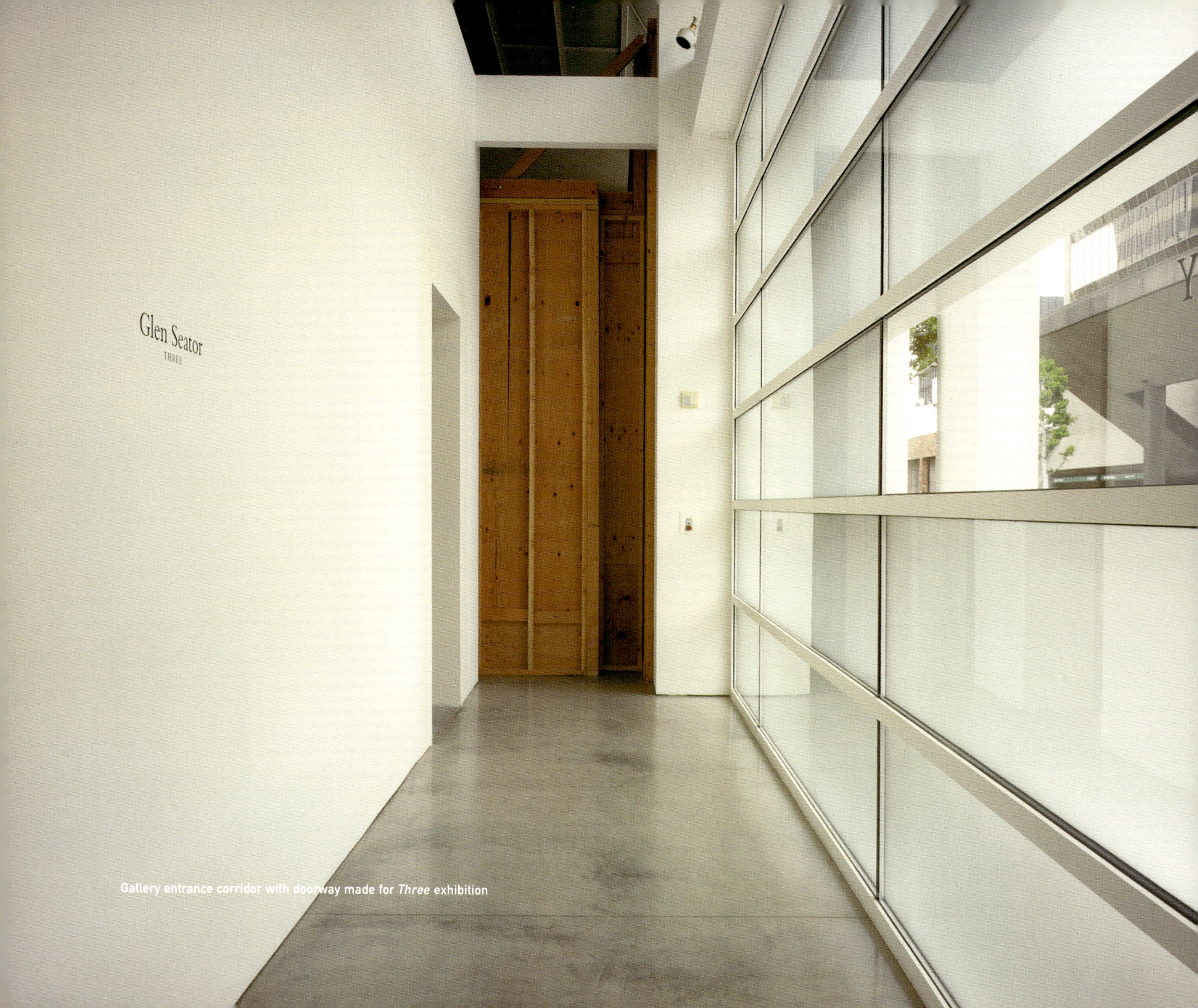

Gallery entrance corridor with doorway made for *Three* exhibition

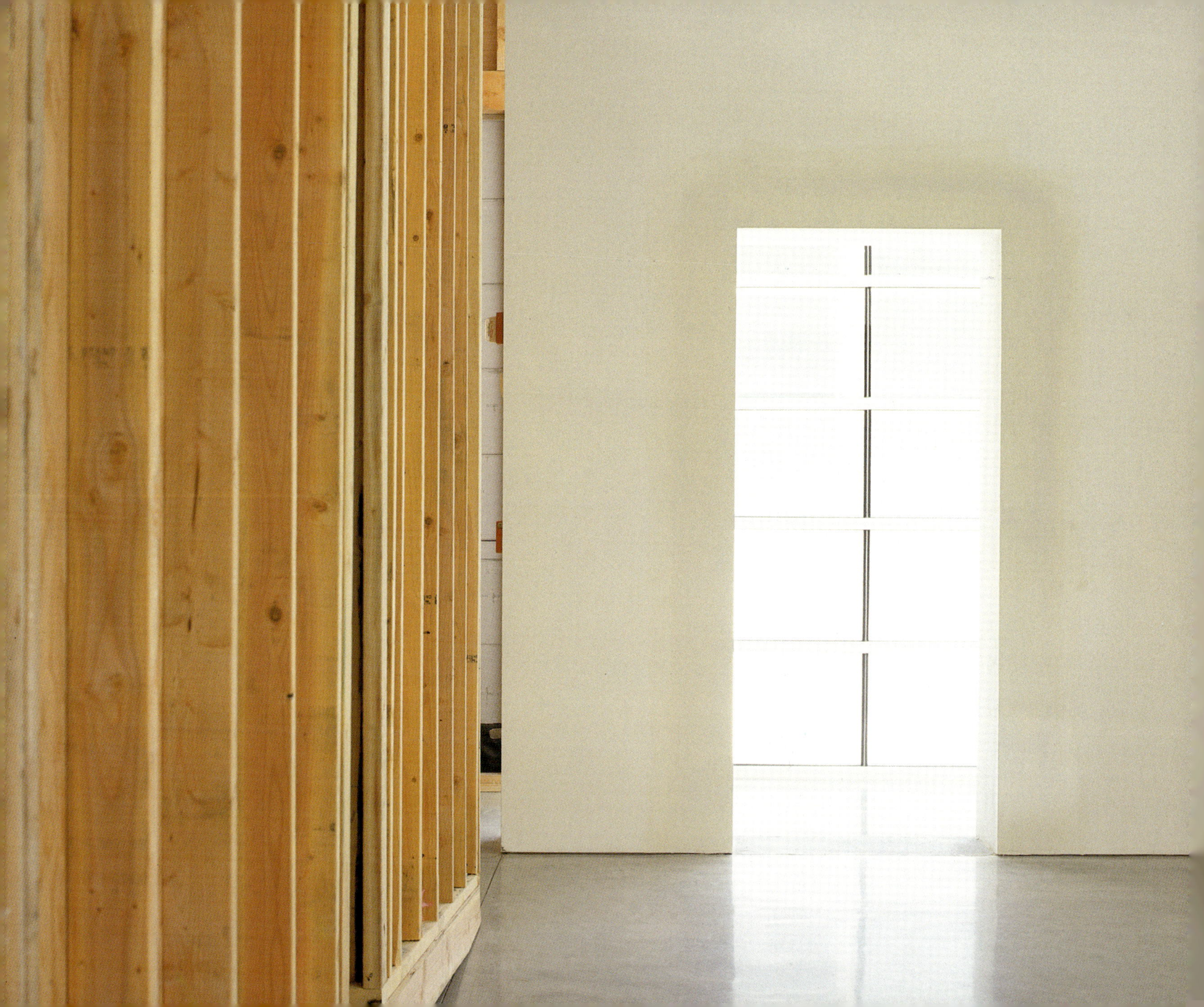

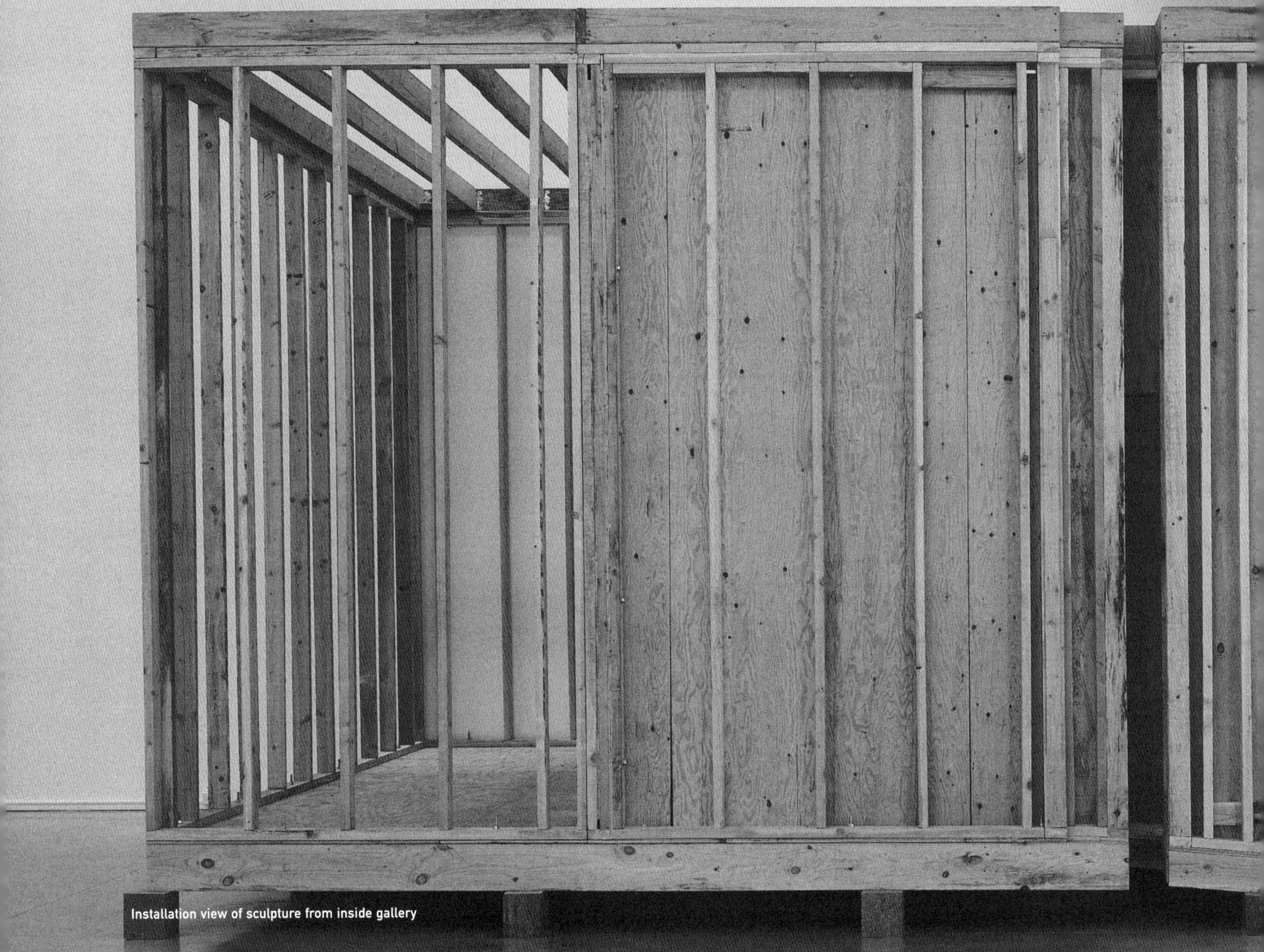

Installation view of sculpture from inside gallery

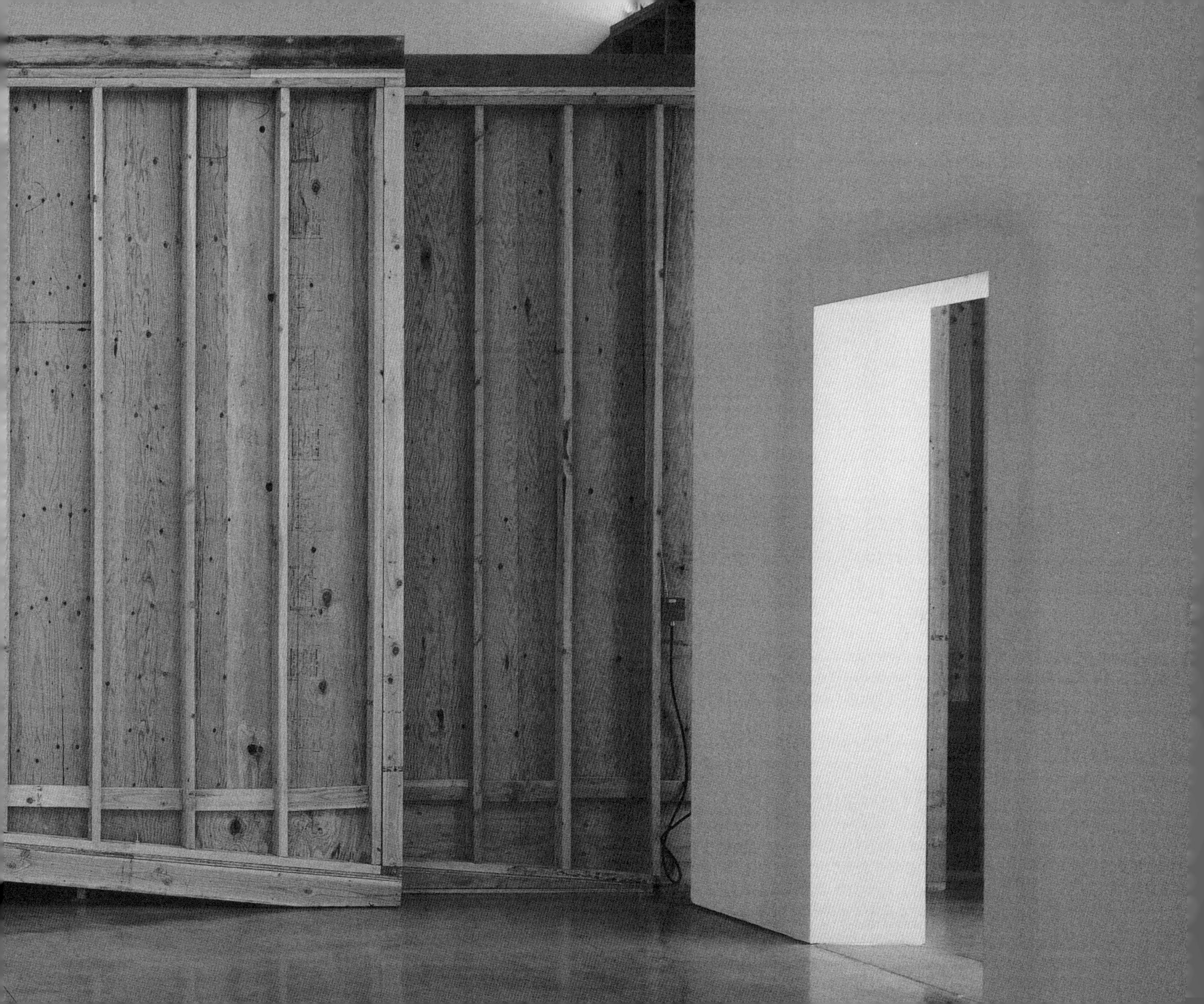

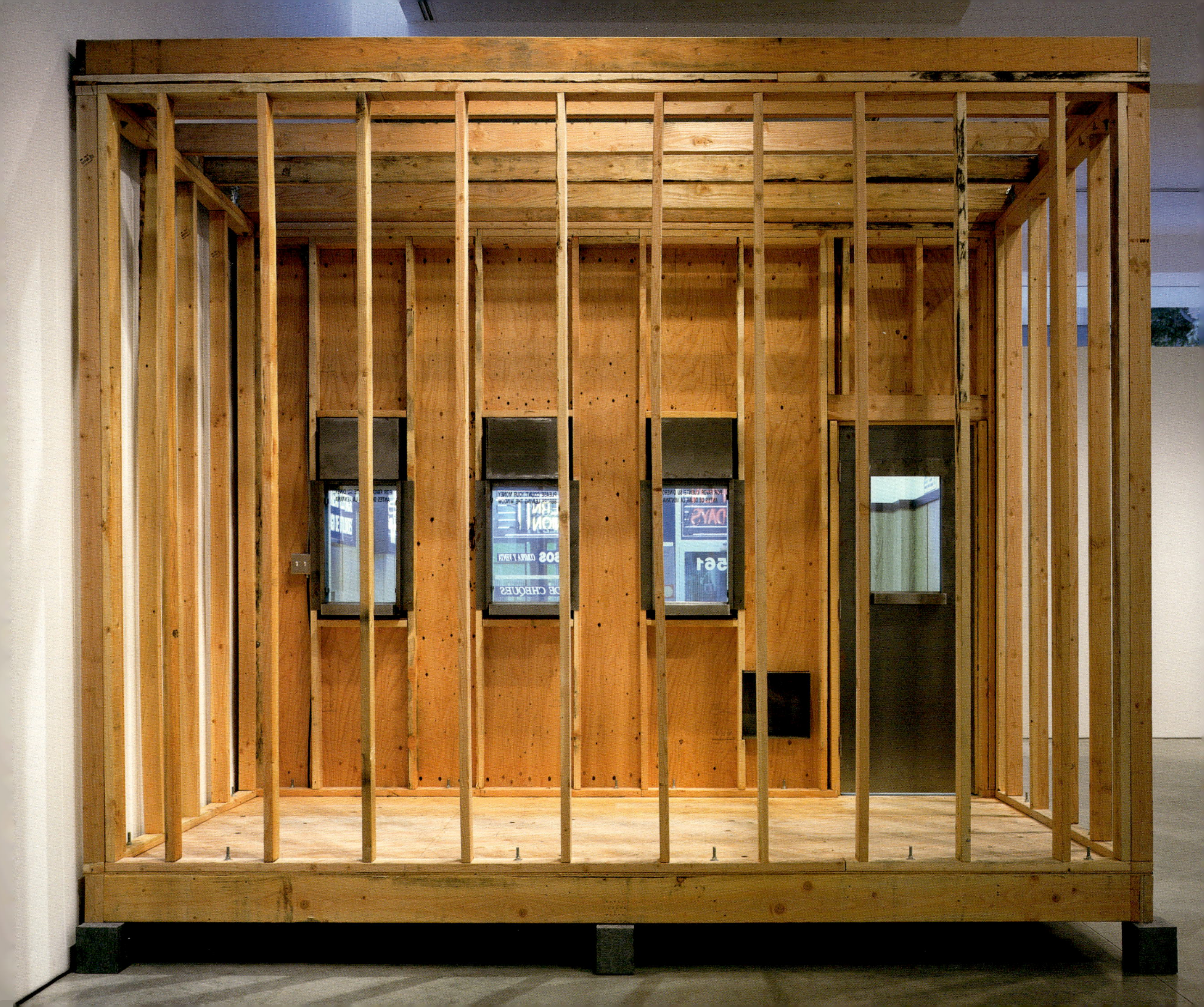

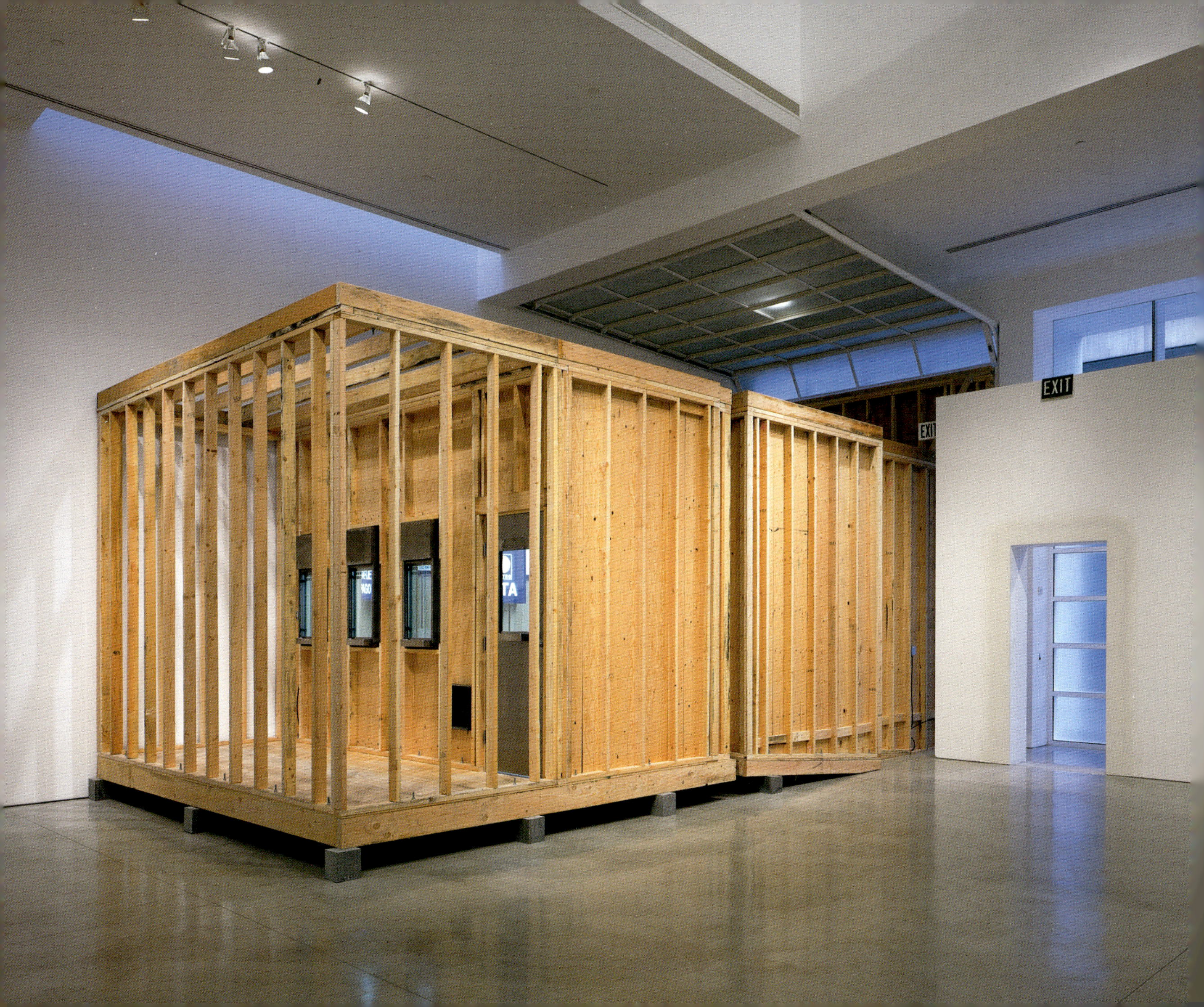

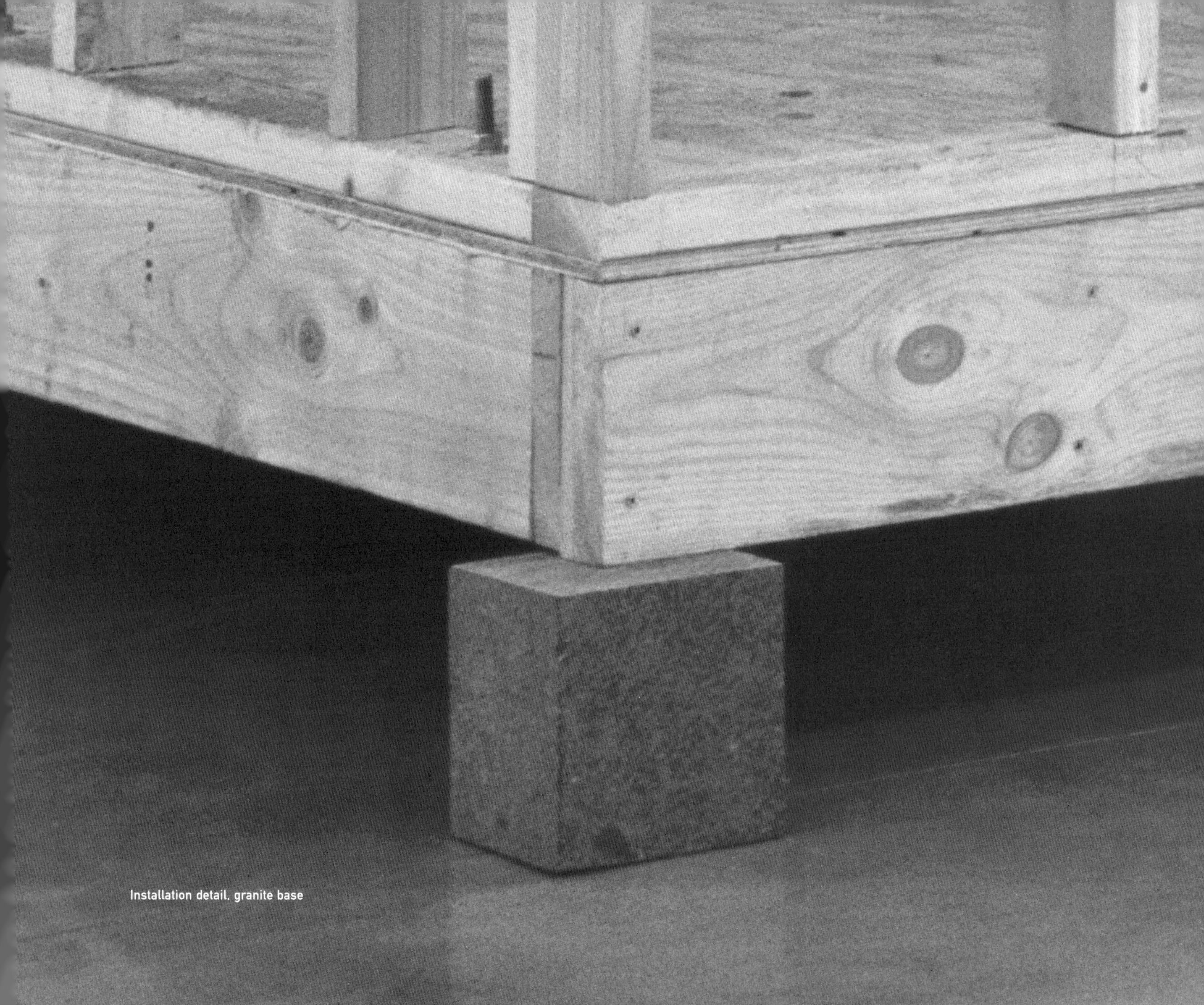

Installation detail, granite base

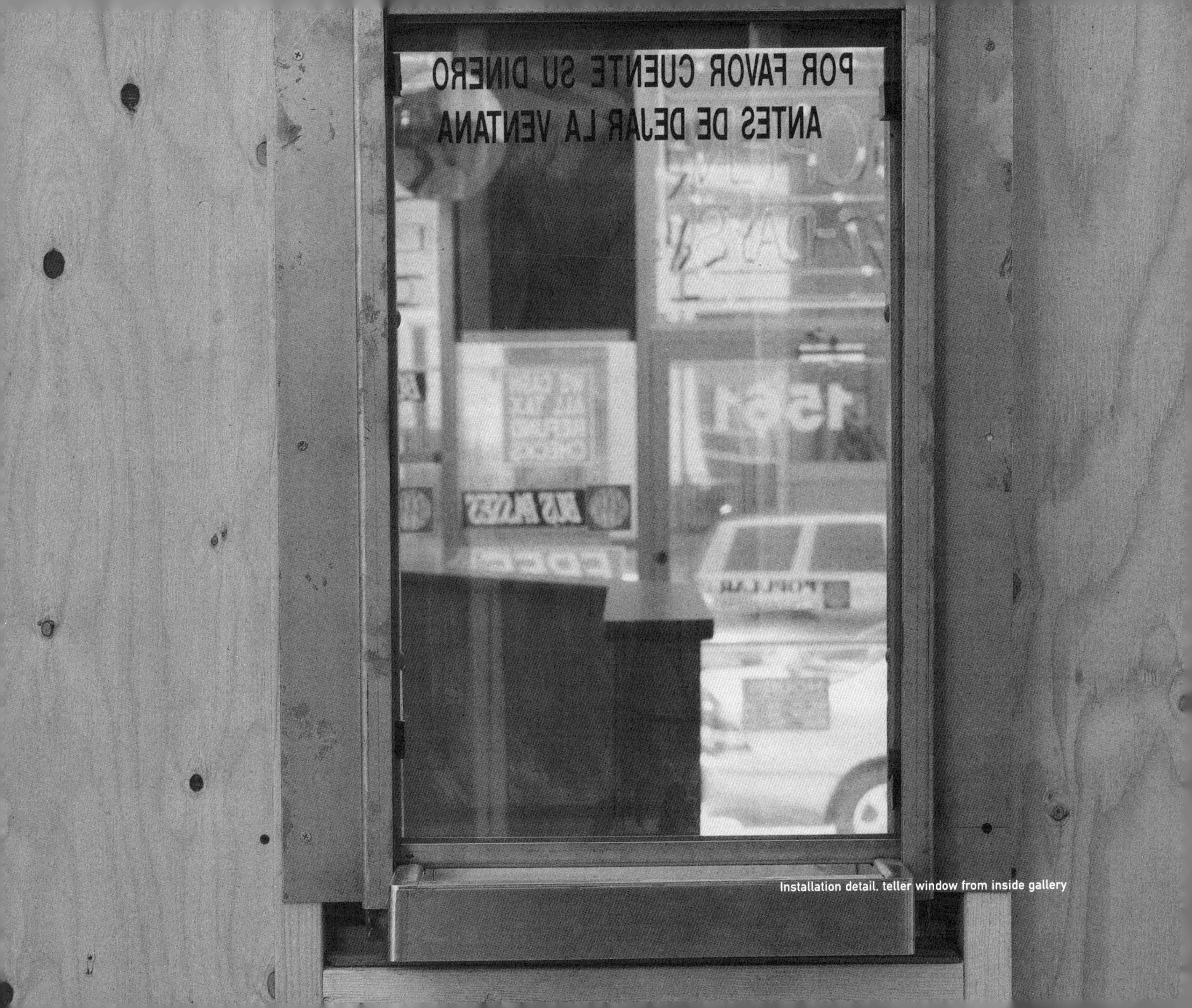

Installation detail, teller window from inside gallery

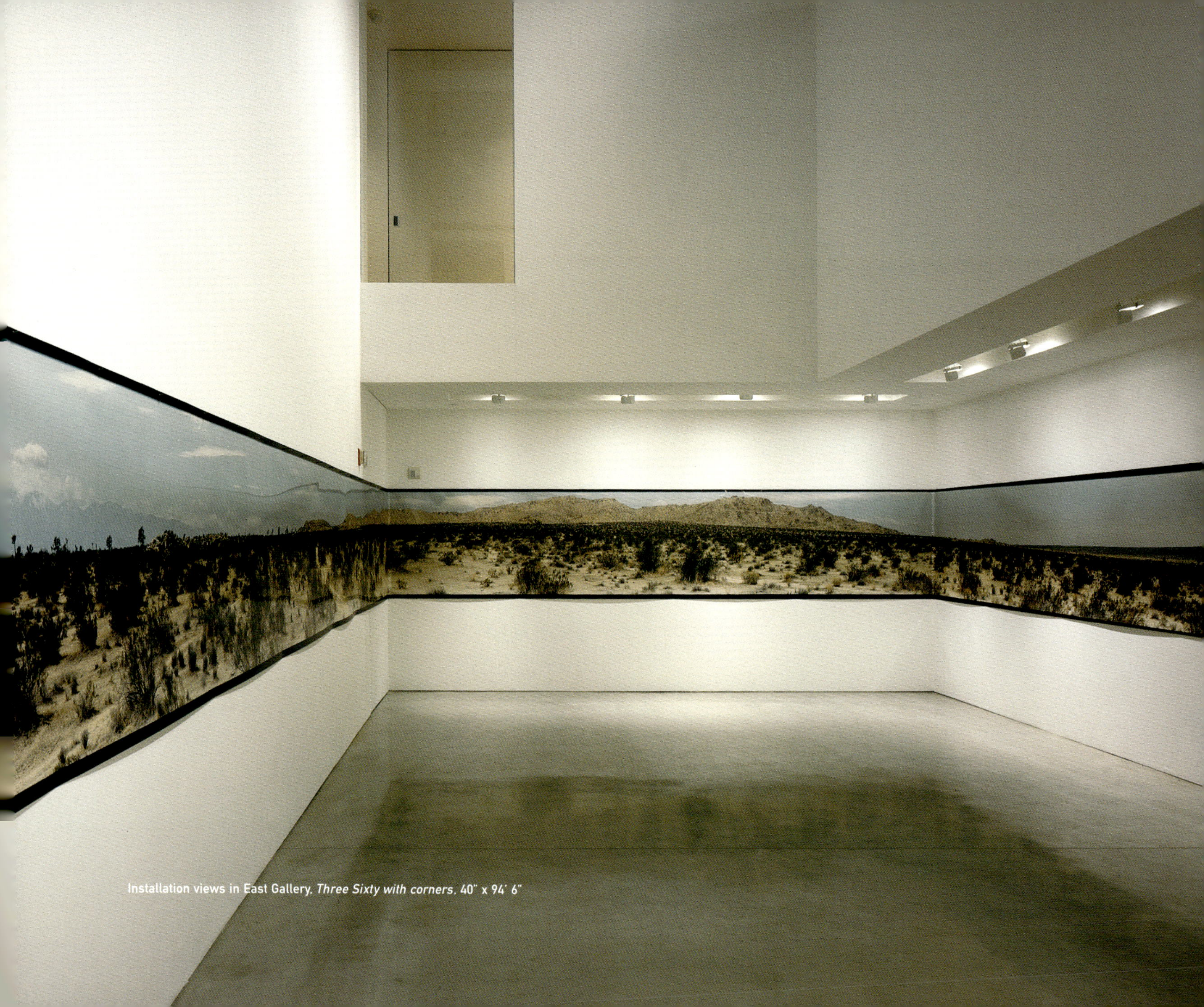

Installation views in East Gallery, *Three Sixty with corners.* 40" x 94' 6"

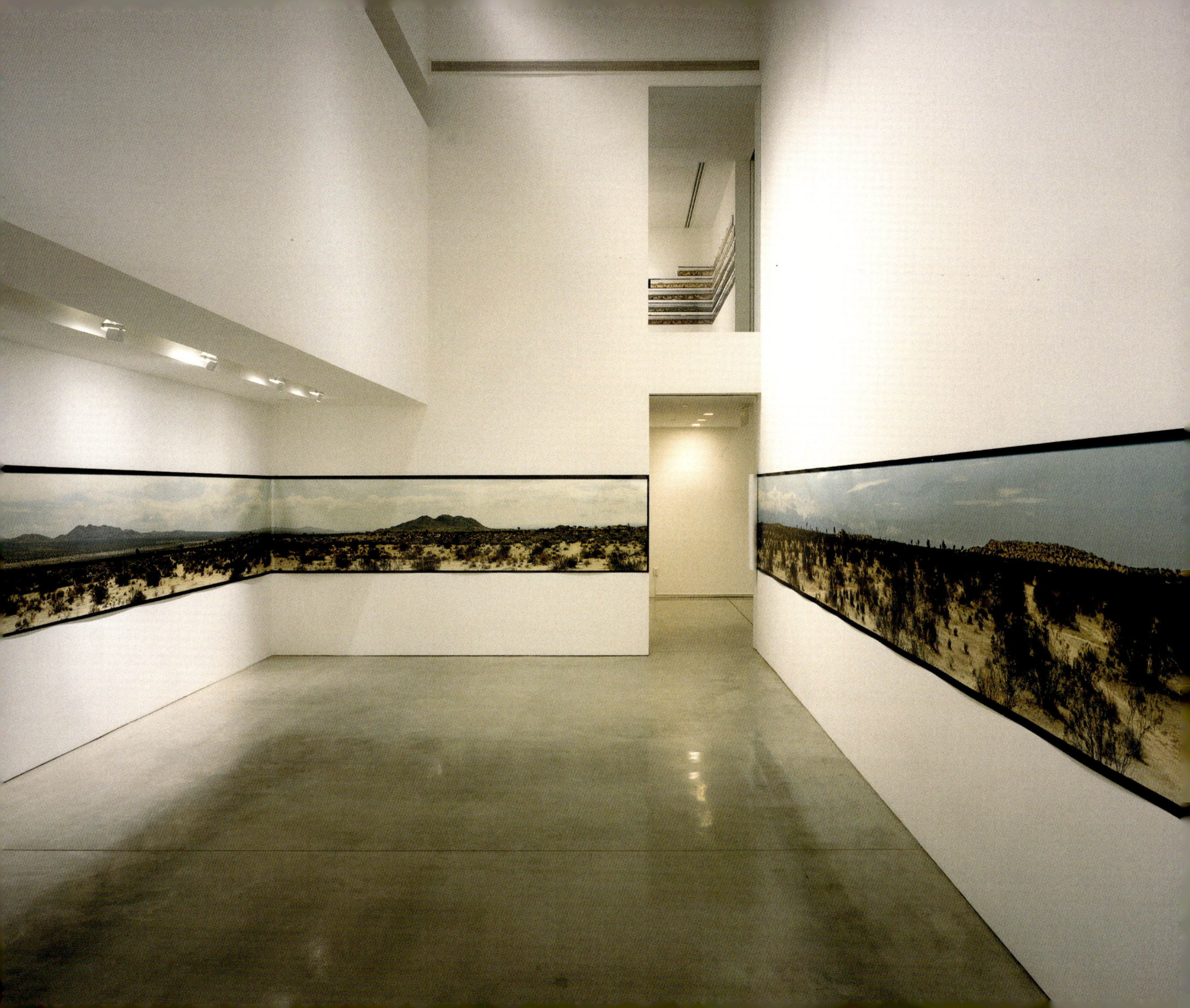

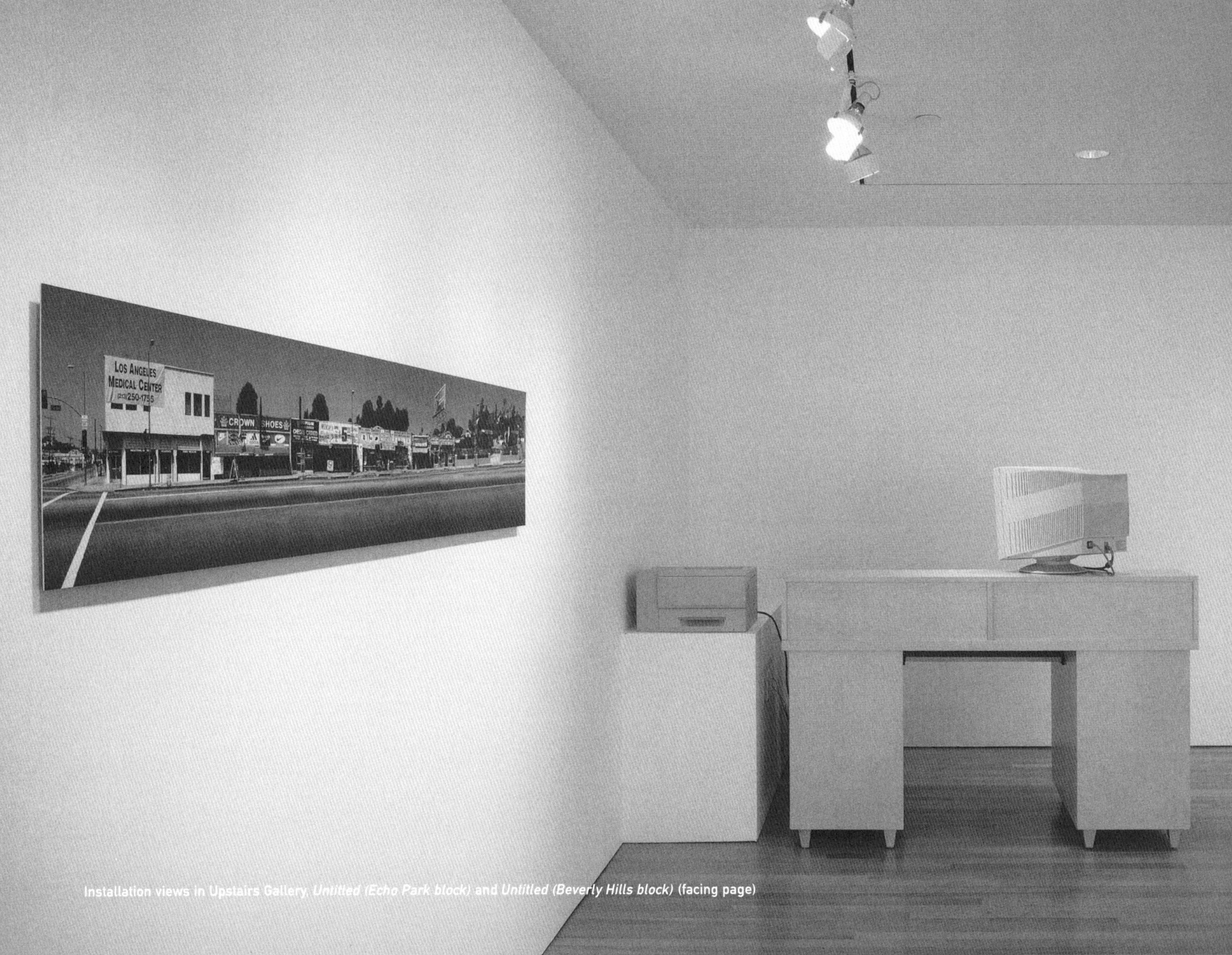

Installation views in Upstairs Gallery, *Untitled (Echo Park block)* and *Untitled (Beverly Hills block)* (facing page)

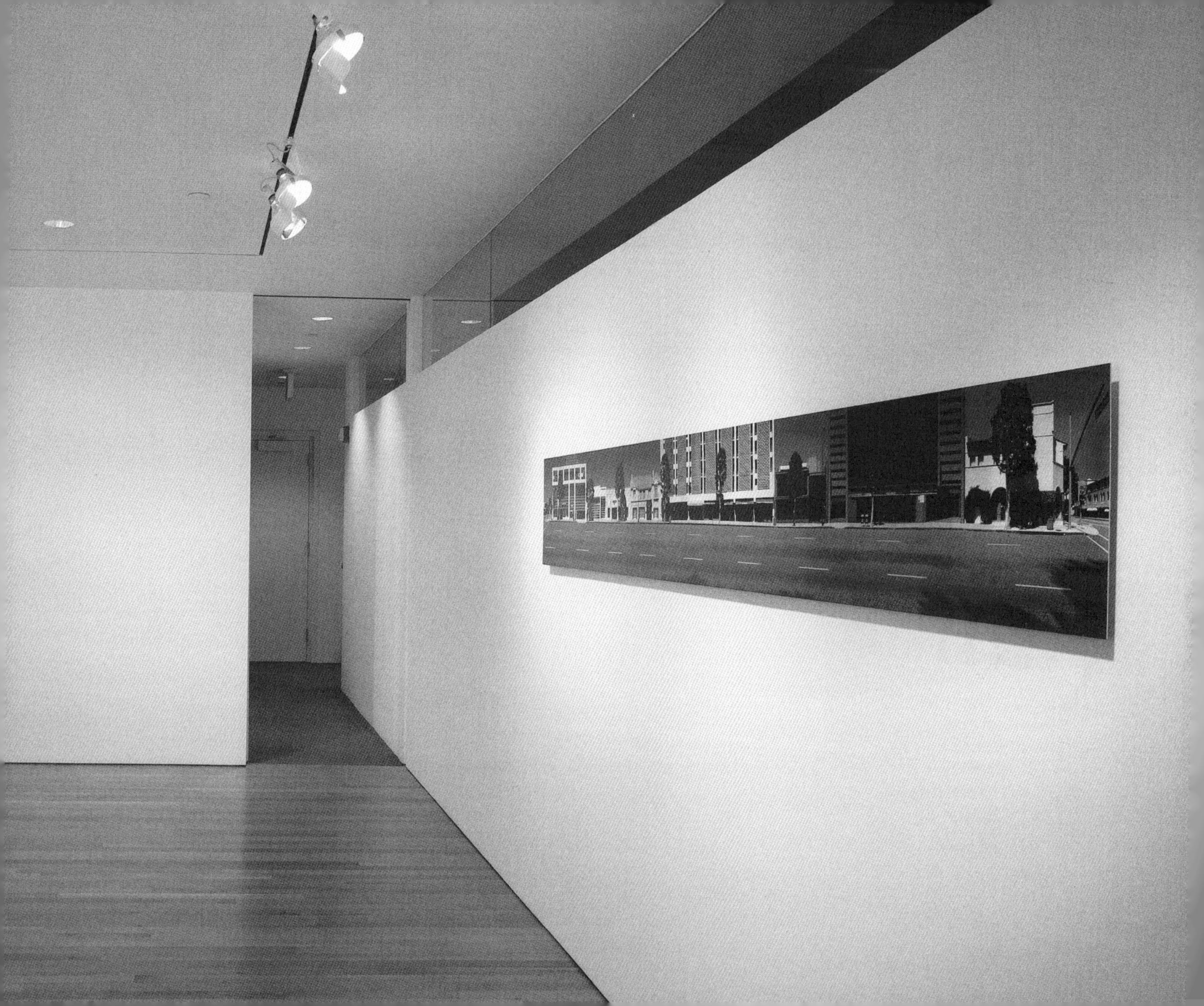

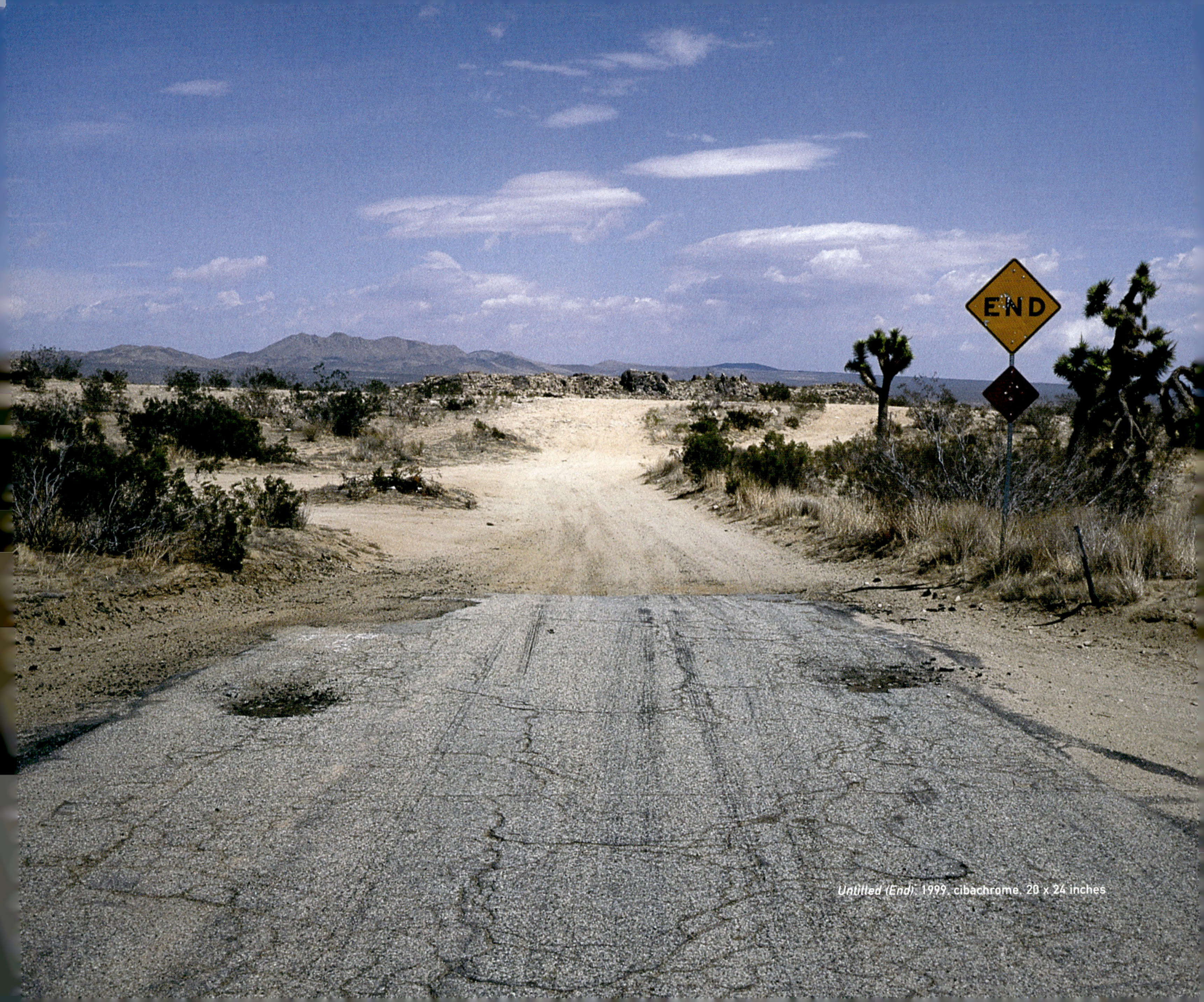

Untitled (End), 1999, cibachrome, 20 x 24 inches

KINESTHETIC CAPITAL: GLEN SEATOR'S *THREE*

David Joselit

I.

In Glen Seator's exhibition *Three* a replica of Popular Cash Express, a sign-encrusted check cashing store in the Eastside Los Angeles neighborhood of Echo Park, is inserted into Gagosian Gallery's hushed and elegant facade in Beverly Hills. Like any other business on North Camden Drive you can enter through the door of this reconstructed storefront which is titled *Fifteen Sixty One* after the address of its model on Sunset Boulevard. Inside all of the attached fixtures of the displaced business are recreated but none of its ephemeral contents: the cash windows opposite the door are not manned by the employees who serve a Latino clientele across town in Echo Park but give a view into the bright modernist interior of the gallery beyond. To enter this exhibition space a visitor must exit the work and walk one door down to a different address, Gagosian's main entrance. Despite the fact that *Fifteen Sixty One* will be dismantled after the exhibition closes, it looks and feels permanent: its architectural elements are not *simulated* like a theater set, but fully constructed. The signmaker for Popular Cash Express has made the signs and Los Angeles Bullet Proof Equipment Company has agreed to provide bullet proof glass and deal trays that would dispense money. Everything in Seator's work conspires to suggest a kind of super or social realism as though time has been stopped momentarily, but will soon resume. But it is precisely this density of detail which gives force to a countervailing effect of disorientation or vertigo. For despite the accuracy of its execution, *Fifteen Sixty One*

is not a simple act of reproduction. Its structure parallels those operations which Freud identified as fundamental to the grammar of dreams: condensation and displacement. In Seator's installation reality is folded over itself and knotted. The spectator is able to carefully scrutinize—and to literally inhabit—the space of dreams, which in ordinary life is as difficult as grasping a fistful of water.

According to the psychoanalysts J. Laplanche and J.-B. Pontalis, psychic *condensation* occurs when "a sole idea represents several associative chains at whose point of intersection it is located," and *displacement* refers to "the fact that an idea's emphasis, interest or intensity is liable to be detached from it and to pass onto other ideas, which were originally of little intensity but were related to the first idea by a chain of associations."[1] In Seator's work both of these mental operations are demonstrated spatially, *but without losing their psychic dimension*. The transposition of the Echo Park Store (which appears only as a box with exposed studs from the interior of the gallery) collapses the Westside and the Eastside of Los Angeles as it elides sculpture with architecture. Similarly, the spatial displacement from Echo Park to Beverly Hills (a particularly charged trajectory given the xenophobia of Los Angeles) serves to project the *visible* economy of transferring money from the U.S. to Latin America which the check cashing store embodies onto the equally global economy which fuels Beverly Hills, but which, in this affluent city, is hidden behind the bland glamor of a generalized historical pastiche. *Fifteen Sixty One* is the architectural version of a slip of the tongue, or a return of the repressed. It is a kind of architectural unconscious.

Seator's art has long sought to mobilize the *unconscious of space* by unveiling the invisible or repressed processes which produce sites materially as rooms and socially as institutions. His operations on existing architectural environments tend to transpose the "neutral" settings of the art world into organisms whose multiple and intersecting procedures possess a cellular logic of replication. *Balloon Frame*, a 1995 installation at the Kunsthalle Basel[2] is a particularly vivid example of this approach. The work was made in a gallery with sheetrocked walls which Seator enclosed on its fourth side. Into the sheetrock he cut a series of interlocking T-shaped templates from which he folded models of the room itself, alternately turned out onto the floor and held aloft with braces. The skin of the space, peeled off its studs became the substance of the objects held within it, and these objects in turn functioned as scale models of the room in which they stood. As the models emerged in a virtually cancerous profusion, the walls disappeared: representation proceeded through consumption. Such a metaphor of ingestion was extended by allowing the by-products of the process—sweepings of dust and extracted screws—to remain in the room as waste. In this installation the art object is literally—umbilically—connected to the exhibition space of which it is a scale model. Consequently it is neither exclusively a function of its environment, nor an autonomous thing, but both. Moreover by making the work on site and retaining the waste products of his cutting and folding Seator aligns the gallery with an artist's studio. *Balloon Frame* thus performs an extraordinary act of condensation in which the body of architecture—sheetrock, plaster, studs, and screws—emerges simultaneously with its colonization as institutional space.

II.

In many of Seator's installations, as in *Balloon Frame*, an art object is constituted by establishing an articulation between an environment and its model, or in different terms, between the real and its representation. An infinite regress is established in which experience and its replication rebound upon one another. *Preventative Measures*, a 1994 installation at The National Gallery of Contemporary Art in Warsaw produced this condition in a particularly acute way. In this project Seator covered the walls, windows and floor of a grand neoclassical gallery with strips of masking tape, lending the vast room the generalized appearance of a pasteboard model. The uncanny result was the sensation of occupying two spaces at once: the thing and its representation. This simultaneity of experience and its doubling as form is what I understand to be Seator's exploration of the architectural unconscious. Since 1990 he has developed a range of strategies for evoking such disruptions. In addition to the umbilical production of models from the space itself (*Balloon Frame*) and the transformation of surface accomplished in *Preventative Measures*, he has tipped full-scale models of administrative offices at precipitous angles in the exhibition areas of Burnett Miller Gallery (Los Angeles), The New York Kunsthalle and the Whitney Museum of American Art, and he has displaced facades or streetscapes from an exterior to an interior at Capp Street Project in San Francisco and White Cube Gallery in London. In the tipped works viewers regularly experience extreme kinesthetic disorientation verging on nausea. These rotated rooms warp space in such a way as to rob the spectator of his or her bearings. On the other hand the displaced street and facade induce sensations of déjà vu, a disorientation which is temporal rather than kinesthetic. As one critic put it, "visually, these works are equivalent to a skip in a record."[3] *Three* introduces a new paradigm of spatial manipulation in Seator's art which draws its force not from the return of the same, as in the San Francisco and

London projects, but from the collapse of difference—differences of space, ethnicity and class. He is producing an urban collage from fragments of the city but it shares with the tradition of painterly or photographic collage a jarring note of discord. *Fifteen Sixty One* ruptures the tasteful period styles and glass facades of Beverly Hills: in a city famous for its themed architecture (Disneyland, after all is less than an hour to the south), and for its exploitation of Latino labor, this intrusion is alternately charged as transgressive and bitterly comic. But in Beverly Hills, this joke cannot be funny. Here is a passage from the city's Architectural Review code:

> The Council hereby finds that Beverly Hills is internationally known and has become a worldwide synonym for beauty, quality, and value; that by far the largest area of the community is zoned for single-family residences, but a significant part is zoned for apartment, commercial, and industrial uses; that most persons who travel through Beverly Hills or do business in and with Beverly Hills do so in its apartment, commercial, and industrial areas; that there is a tendency of some owners and developers in these areas to disregard beauty and quality in construction and a consequent serious danger that construction of inferior quality and appearance in the apartment, commercial, and industrial areas will degrade and depreciate the image, beauty, and reputation of Beverly Hills...

Three, which required special council approval, evidently hits a nerve. It is an irony worthy of Duchamp that a structure which would be intolerable as architecture in Beverly Hills may be justified only within the category of art.

III.

Los Angeles is a city founded on mobility: the mobility of water required to transform its desert topography into a habitable landscape; the mobility of immigrants from the East and the Midwest, from Latin America and Asia who have made it a cosmopolitan world city; the mobility of capital which enables its entertainment, defense, and high technology industries to flourish; and above all, the mobility of the automobile which facilitates movement across its vast expanse. *Three* accelerates this mobility—and gives it an apocalyptic dimension—by causing facades from opposite ends of the city to collide, conjuring away the intervening neighborhoods of Silver Lake, Los Feliz, Hollywood, and West Hollywood. Like Dorothy's House *Fifteen Sixty One* has landed on the Yellow Brick Road. But this urban collage is complicated by an additional component in the installation—the third of the "three" of its title. On the four walls of Gagosian's back gallery is installed *Three Sixty with corners*, a single wraparound panoramic photographic print of an undeveloped desert landscape taken on the rural outskirts of Los Angeles. In proximity to the cacophony of the installation's streetscape, this image of the vast, dry emptiness from which the restless, ornate city arises has something of the effect of pulling the plug on a thundering sound system: it produces a deafening silence. The city is made to seem miraculous and superfluous at once. But if the desert photograph functions on one register as the blank ground onto which Los Angeles is figured forth, it also domesticates the landscape by transforming it into a room. And more, a room housing a panorama which presumes a single valid viewing position at its center. If the panorama decenters the city's urban collage, it does so by pinning the human subject in place.

Such a dynamic of shifting spatial and conceptual positions in which mobility is suddenly arrested is characteristic of *Three*. Indeed for all its gesturing toward spatial elasticity, the work delivers a series of dead ends.

The recreated store itself is a kind of barricade. It plugs the aperture created by a large roll-up door in the facade of Gagosian whose purpose is to facilitate the transfer of monumental works of art from the street to the gallery. As art, Seator's work is a kind of blockage, but this blockage possesses its own aperture: the door giving access to the ghost interior of *Fifteen Sixty One*. But this too is a false promise: there is no exit onto the gallery space. A parallel promenade of interruptions is established when one enters the gallery's main door. Here the normal path into the large exhibition space is blocked by the exposed exterior of the store which appears to be jammed into the gallery from outside. Access to the exhibition space is given through a new passageway cut into an existing wall, but once inside there is little to see but the closed boxy exterior of the work, raised on plinths. Seator has planned an adventure founded in frustration: every attempt to possess *Three* optically and conceptually is thwarted. Even its third element, the panoptic landscape photograph in the back gallery, underscores this destabilization of spectatorship. The continuous landscape spinning around the room is broken into folds at the four corners of its container, causing the viewer's expectation of unhindered vision to bump up against the geometry of the room—a stop-and-start rhythm which parallels the viewer's progress through and around *Fifteen Sixty One*. Perhaps the pivot of the irreconcilable spatial contradictions established in *Three* is the "sketch" of the teller's area of the Echo Park store which is framed in at the back of the sculpture. This openwork structure—the place where money is dispensed across town—is a third zone, a boundary space where from one perspective, the sculpture may be said to taper off, and from another it seems to gather force.

Three simultaneously produces an accelerated mobility and immobilized states of frustration and blockage. Such a conjunction of opposing velocities may seem paradoxical, but on the contrary, it serves as an accurate portrait of our globalized world in which intense and restless investment can seize on virtually anything as capital (from DNA to garbage) and just as quickly withdraw, rendering businesses, neighborhoods or even nations "residual." Seator's installation is framed by alternate representations of financial transfer: a downmarket check cashing store on the one hand and an upmarket gallery on the other. Moreover the image of the former is presented as the product of the latter (after all this work is for sale). The space of the check cashing store is rendered obsolete or residual, and yet its representation as a sculpture puts it back into circulation in a different economy of meaning. Seator does not simply *illustrate* such shifts, he evokes their violence: the vertiginous jumps and halts of valuation and re-valuation. In other words he makes the veiled spatial operations of global capital kinesthetically immediate. *Three* was made for Gagosian Gallery, but the work is fabricated so that it may be installed elsewhere. To think of this fiercely site-specific work uprooted and reframed inevitably induces melancholy, and yet I wonder if its force will be even greater when it undergoes a second order of displacement. In a different place it will truly function as a floating residue—the deserted camp of capital which is always somewhere else.

[1] J. Laplanche and J.-B. Pontalis, *The Language of Psycho-Analysis*, translated by Donald Nicholson-Smith. New York: W.W. Norton and Company, 1973, pp. 82 and 120.

[2] This work is an expanded version of a piece presented at White Columns in New York in 1992.

[3] John Slyce, "Glen Seator, White Cube Gallery," *What's On* (August 27, 1997): p. 16.

David Joselit is associate professor in the Department of Art History at the University of California Irvine. He is author of *Infinite Regress: Marcel Duchamp: 1910-1941* and writes regularly on contemporary art and culture.

BIOGRAPHY

SELECTED GROUP EXHIBITIONS

1998   *View Two*, Mary Boone Gallery, New York

1997   *1997 Whitney Biennial*, Whitney Museum of American Art, New York
     curated by Lisa Phillips and Louise Neri

     Broken Home, Greene Naftali Gallery, New York
     curated by Caroline Schneider and Meg O'Rourke

1996   *The Palace of Good Luck*, Burnett Miller Gallery, Los Angeles

     Peter Halley / Matthew Ritchie / Glen Seator, Room, New York
     curated by Owen Drolet

1995   *Critical Distance*, Neuberger Museum of Art, Purchase, New York
     curated by Cornelia Butler

     Construction Process VI, The International Artists' Museum, Mitzpe Ramon, Israel

     Material Matters: Art at the Anchorage, Creative Time Inc., New York

     Patrick Callery, New York

1994   *Vienna / New York*, 163 Mercer Street, New York
     curated by Warren Niestuchowski

1993   *Construction in Process IV: My Home is Your Home*, The International Artists' Museum, Lodz, Poland
     organized by Ryszard Wasko

     Sleepless Nights, Auditorium Project, PS1 Museum, The Institute for Contemporary Art, New York
     curated by Zdenka Gabalova

1992   *Mssrs B.'s Curio Shop*, Threadwaxing Space, New York
     curated by Saul Ostrow

     Update '92, White Columns, New York

1989   *Before or After Form or Function?*, White Columns, New York

     Pb: Works on Lead, Nohra Haime Gallery, New York

PUBLIC COLLECTIONS

     The Solomon R. Guggenheim Museum

     The Whitney Museum of American Art

SELECTED BIBLIOGRAPHY

Marcoci, R. and Murphy, D., *New Art*, Harry N. Abrams, New York, New York, 1997 (photo)

Barrett, David, "Glen Seator, White Cube", *Art Monthly*, September, 1997, pp. 35-36

Kent, Sarah, "Glen Seator, White Cube", *Time Out*, August 20-27, 1997 (photo)

Slyce, John, "Glen Seator, White Cube Gallery", *What's On*, August 27, 1997 p.16 (photo)

Feaver, William, "Frankly, this place is going down the pan", *The Observer Review*, July 20, 1997

Danto, Arthur C., "Whitney Biennial Review", *The Nation*, May/June 1997

Schumacher, Donna, "Glen Seator, Capp Street Project", *ARTnews*, Summer 1997, p.142 (photo)

Yablonsky, Linda, "Showtime at the Whitney", *Time Out NY*, April 3-10, 1997, pp.39-40 (photo)

Sabine, Russ, "Glen Seator, Ein Portrait", *Neu Bildende Kunst*, March-April 1997, p. 59-64 (photos)

Kimmelman, Michael, "Narratives Snagged on the Cutting Edge", *New York Times*, March 21, 1997, p. C1 (photo)

Knight, Christopher, "Show Time at Biennial: Send in the Big Crowds", *Los Angeles Times*, March 21, 1997

Arning, Bill, "Biennial Best", *Paper Magazine*, March 1997 (photo)

Finkel, Jori, "Over There", *Express*, February 28, 1997, p. 39

Eggers, Dave, "Perfect", *SFWeekly*, February 19-25, 1997, p. 55 (photos)

Friedman, Roberto, "Concrete Poetry", *Bay Area Report*, February 20, 1997, p. 52 (photo)

Bonetti, David, "Gallery Watch", *San Francisco Examiner*, February 7, 1997, p. 14 (photo)

Garchik, Leah, "Masters of the Pavement", *San Francisco Chronicle*, February 7, 1997, p. 20 (photo)

Baker, Kenneth, "Genuine Street Art", *San Francisco Chronicle*, February 1, 1997, pp. E1/E2 (photos)

Koplos, Janet, "Glen Seator at The New York Kunsthalle", *Art in America*, February 1997 (photo)

Vogel, Carol, "Inside Art: Entering a Charmed Circle", *The New York Times*, January 3, 1997

Shottenkirk, Dena, "Glen Seator, New York Kunsthalle", *World Art*, Winter 1996 (photos)

Drolet, Owen, "Ouveture: Glen Seator", *Flash Art*, November/December 1996 (photos)

"Centerfold: Glen Seator", *Bomb Magazine*, Winter 1996/1997 (photos)

Quinn, Jonathan, "Time Out at the Kunstraum Wien (De-constructed and Constructive)", *The Vienna Reporter*, July 1996 (photo)

Pagel, David, "Lots of Luck", *The Los Angeles Times*, July 25, 1996

"Highlights: Glen Seator", *Die Presse*, July 22, 1996

Metzger, Rainer, "Kunstraum: Zum Schluß ein Schluß Humor", *Der Standard*, June 20, 1996

Arning, Bill, "Down for the Kunst", *Time Out NY*, June 7-12, 1996 (photo)

Levin, Kim, "Art Short List: 29'0''", *The Village Voice*, May 14, 1996 (photo)

Auerbach, Lisa Anne, "Glen Seator, Burnett Miller Gallery", *Artforum*, March 1996 (photo)

Kugelman, Kerry, "Glen Seator at Burnett Miller", *Art Issues*, #42, March/April 1996 (photo)

Brüderlin, Markus, *Herausgeber Kunstraum Wien*, 1996, exhibition series catalogue, pp. 96, 113-115 (photos)

Brüderlin, Markus, "Die Transformation des White Cube", epilogue to

O'Doherty, Brian, *In der Weisen Zelle (Inside Inside the White Cube)*, ed. Kemp, Wolfgang, Merve, Berlin, 1996, p. 163

Pagel, David, "Seator's Cabinet Holds a Mix of Fun, Seriousness", *Los Angeles Times*, Calendar Section, December 7, 1995

"Buzz Bets – Home Improvements", *Buzz Magazine*, December 1995 / January 1996 (photo)

Yau, John, *Material Matters*, Creative Time Inc., 1995 (illustrated catalog)

Pagel, David, "Israel FAX", *Art Issues*, #40, November 1995 (photo)

Bayliss, Sarah, "Construction in Process V", *World Art*, October 1995 (photo)

Drolet, Owen, "Construction in Process V", *Zingmagazine*, NY, Autumn 1995 (photo)

Grunenberg, Christoph, and Kellein, Thomas, *Balloon Frame*, Kunsthalle Basel, Basel, Switzerland, 1995 (illustrated catalogue, exhibition series)

Butler, Cornelia, *Critical Distance: Between Art and Architecture*, Neuberger Museum of Art, SUNY, Purchase, NY, 1995 (brochure with photos)

Zimmer, William, "Neuberger's Anniversary Exhibit", *The New York Times*, February 5, 1995, p.16 (photo)

"Incarnations", *New Observations*, #105, March-April 1995, p. 27 (photo)

Schwendenwein, Jude, "Collectors", *Sculpture*, January-February 1995, p. 18 (photo)

Volk, Gregory, & Ostrow, Saul, *Glen Seator*, National Gallery of Contemporary Art, Warsaw (28 pages, photos)

Arning, Bill, *Update '92*, White Columns, 1992 (photo)

Levin, Kim, "Sleepless Nights", *The Village Voice*, February 24, 1993, p. 61

Smith, Roberta, "The Curio Shop", *The New York Times*, 1992

Ostrow, Saul, *Mssr. B.'s Curio Shop*, New York, 1992 (illustrated catalog)

Hirsh, David, "Glen Seator at White Columns", *New York Native*, April 5, 1992

GLEN SEATOR'S DARING DESIRING-MACHINES

Terry R. Myers

Do not use thought to ground a political practice in Truth; nor political action to discredit, as mere speculation, a line of thought. Use political practice as an intensifier of thought, and analysis as a multiplier of the forms and domains for the intervention of political action.

— Michel Foucault, "Preface" to Gilles Deleuze and Félix Guattari's *Anti-Oedipus: Capitalism and Schizophrenia*[1]

He who has once begun to open the fan of memory never comes to the end of its segments; no image satisfies him, for he has seen that it can be unfolded, and only in its folds does the truth reside; that image, that taste, that touch for whose sake all this has been unfurled and dissected; and now remembrance advances from small to smallest details, from the smallest to the infinitesimal, while that which it encounters in these microcosms grows ever mightier.

— Walter Benjamin, "A Berlin Chronicle"[2]

It is rare to find work at the end of this century that accepts and fulfills the promise of (self-)criticality by asserting boldly—in form, content, and context—that the hilarious, even lunatic thrill of art itself is *not* gone; there is valuable work still to be done with *more* rather than less. During the last decade, Glen Seator has developed a way of working with materials that can best be described as "complicating" in the most galvanizing sense of the word: more often than not, just when you think you've got your head around one of his projects, it goes somewhere—or does (or looks like) something—*else*. Such a practice, of course, is locatable in the territory scouted by the likes of Deleuze & Guattari in *Anti-Oedipus*: "It is at work everywhere, functioning smoothly at times, at other times in fits and starts. It breathes, it heats, it eats. It shits and fucks. What a mistake to have ever said *the* id. Everywhere *it* is machines—real ones, not figurative ones: machines driving other machines, machines being driven by other machines, with all the necessary couplings and connectors."[3] Seator's works are "desiring-machines" in the best of ways: in terms of not only how much they (mis)behave like the body (especially in how they can make our own bodies act up or out), but also how provocatively and effortlessly (such ease being an absolute shock here) they connect and couple with those multiple histories, sites, and situations that provoke and sustain both poetics and politics.

As a thoughtful and unanxious observer of the achievements, accidents and failures of the late modernist sculptural practice, post-studio production, and site/non-site specificity of the late 1960s and early 1970s, Seator has distinguished himself from most of his peers in his commitment to what should be understood as a demonstration of *agility* rather than power (or the rhetoric of power[4]): a flexibility in the face of late (or so-called global) capitalism, a fluidity that infiltrates and dilutes the hypocrisies infecting social discourse, a balancing act of surprisingly human proportions at a critical moment in history. It can now be said that what can be doubly called the "stance" of Seator's work is a complete position of *accommodation*, not one of giving in, but rather *out*.

Given recent art history, it is not surprising that such potent exteriorizing was first played out by Seator inside his studio with a distinct series of everyday activities, "jobs" that he continues to produce not only on their own circumscribed terms, but also as the physical and conceptual framework for his larger endeavors. More like Bruce Nauman than Michael Asher, for Seator these activities are grounded in a studio-as-laboratory, a non-institutional space where components of a daily routine are "tested" for their abilities to maintain a critically interstitial presence while remaining formally and referentially equivalent to each other as art. Mindful of how (post-) minimalist methodology moved quickly away from "formless" works like Richard Serra's *Splashing*, 1968, to the cleanliness of so-called high minimalism, and clearly aware of a late-1980s scatter art phenomenon that was retracing certain steps on its way to becoming increasingly "well-placed" as well, Seator deliberately organized his studio activities around

performing a mess and cleaning it up, *almost*. He has described his method as "following set procedure and trying to keep a straight face,"[5] a statement of purpose that is grounded in a political refusal to laugh at the joke.

More than aware of the psychoanalytic fixations on notions of "lack," and skeptical of the ways in the early 1990s in which such absence was being allowed presence in art production in terms of identity politics,[6] Seator—not unlike Felix Gonzalez-Torres (who once said "I always said I wanted to be a spy"[7])—"hid" consequential things in plain sight, making what on first viewing looked like classic process work (in other words, to a certain extent, work that remains *blank*), yet without the displacement, removal, and denial. (To *not* do these things requires what Seator calls a "retraining"—note the absence of the word "sublimation.") *Failed Repair (Spill #4 and #5)*, 1990, for example, is comprised of two rectilinear openings in a wall—a horizontal one at head level, and a vertical one waist-high—through which the artist poured from behind the amount of plaster needed to fill the opening. Very much "failed repairs," as he calls them, they are completely successful in their "orificial" excesses, much more than mere slips.

While much less visceral than the spills, Seator's other studio activities—specifically sweeping, pouring and wallraising—maintain their solvent relationships to the body in situations purposefully left susceptible to other types of spatial disruptions (driven home in his large-scale projects):

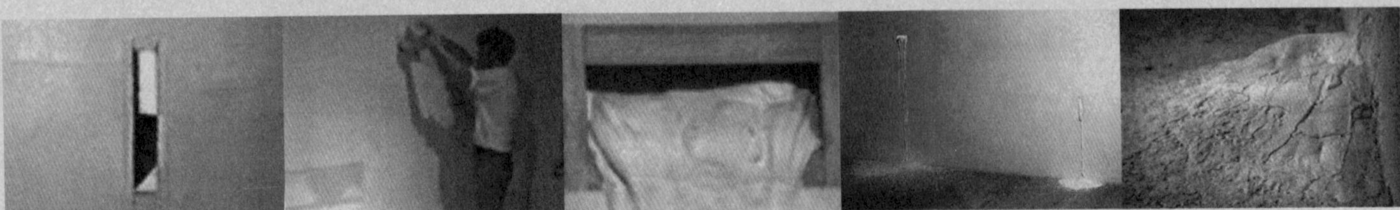

Failed Repair (Spill #4 and #5), 1990 (remade 1992), video stills

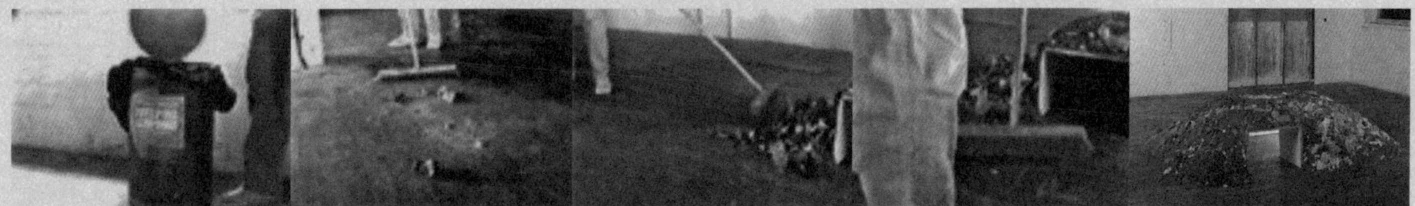

symbolic shifts in scale and position, inversions and revisions of site-specificity, exchanges and displacements that are both photographic and cinematic in nature. Like the spills, the works made from these slightly-more-controlled studio activities leave out the last step: the removal. *Untitled (Interrupted Sweeping)*, 1991-95, is one version of an ongoing work in which Seator uses sweeping compound to accomplish the daily activity of getting the studio back in shape. The intended purpose of the compound—to help pick up *everything* on the floor—benefits the art here, because it does that and more, adding itself to the debris as form and content. At the end, the remains of the day are left undisposed, held in a curiously perpetual state of interruption, piled on top of a small jerry-rigged model of the space itself made from pieces of sheetrock cut from the walls.

Such tensile self-reflexiveness is echoed in another ongoing series of *Planned Puddles*: works in which the floor plan of the space is incised into the floor, and the surrounding flooring is raised to create a shallow vessel that is then sealed with silicone. The resulting receptacle is filled with some type of liquid: white wall paint (kept wet), detergent, or, most suggestive, the (dirty) water used to clean the space—creating a fluid, yet almost photographically stilled and reflective surface that mirrors the space it represents schematically. A type of (thumbnail, snapshot?) portraiture that allows the viewers to "get" the room in one glance, the puddles picture a simultaneous "before-and-after" effect that relies upon their subject itself (the space) in a unusual truth-to-materials manner. What we have here is a room looking at an image of itself as a part of itself. (The implications of this approach would be extended in much different terms

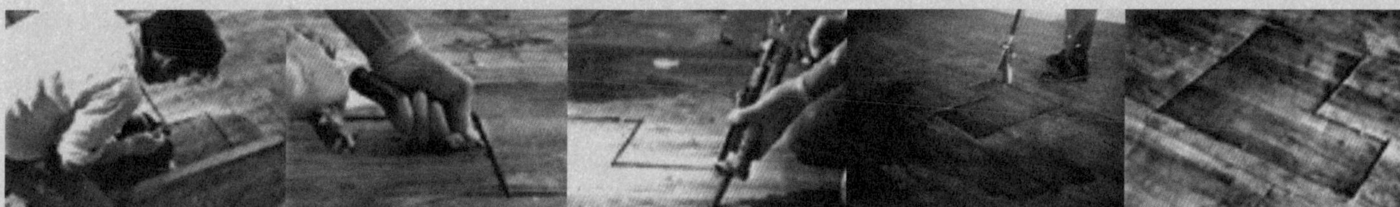

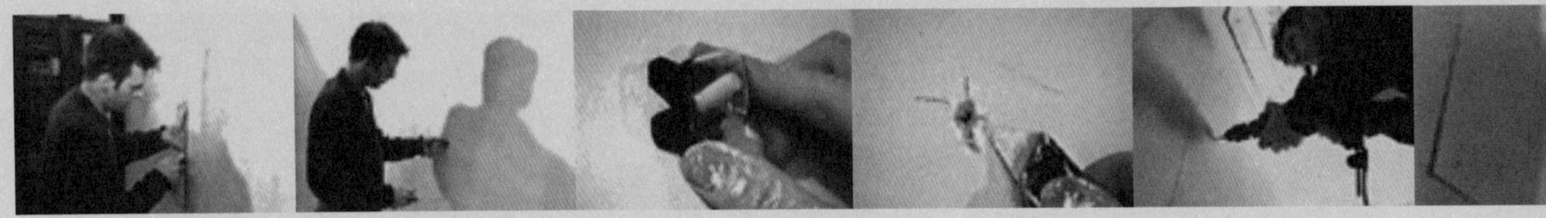

in *Preventative Measures*, 1994, an installation in which a salon in Warsaw's National Gallery of Contemporary Art (Zaçheta) was transformed by Seator into an ethereal yet overwhelming image of itself by 8000 square feet of masking tape.)

Seator's wallraisings take things even further, moving from the pictorial situation of the puddles into what is often called (strangely here) "relief": a contingency in which a mapping of a space emerges from what looks like the first steps towards the deconstructive undoing of the room itself. It is a release of pressure, if you will, that has been provided by two sets of pointed actions: a surgical, potentially violent incision into a real wall delineated in the plan itself; and a discovery, excavation, and loosening of the screws and seams underneath its surface. Made completely from the materials of the "original" construction, the wallraisings can be re-absorbed into the site at any time, not unlike ghosts in the machine, present in their absence.

If we accept Seator's idea that an act of retraining is required to resist or refuse the negative production of lack, then it should come as no surprise that what can be thought of as the "memory-exchange" of a public school gymnasium/auditorium-turned-museum would provide him with his first substantial opportunity to interweave the complexities of his work onto

and into a public/private framework designed to preserve the social borders between interior and exterior (grammar school, of course, being a place of accidents, some of which require such substances as sweeping compound!). *Untitled (Auditorium installation)*, 1993, at PS1, enabled Seator to set in (suspended) motion all of his activities on a major scale. Fundamentally a presentation of the use and wear of the room to itself and its viewers, the project revolved around massive amounts of dirt, most of which had been taken from the surrounding site and packed against the third-floor windows (held in place by sheets of plywood that were cut to leave a gap at the top of each window to let in natural light). The overhead grid of artificial lights were lowered almost to the floor, and each exposed bulb spotlighted a corresponding pile of dirt and sweeping compound that was part of a tangible, residual record of the duration of the exhibition. These lights were then mapped by a analogous set of working fixtures installed vertically on the back side of a wall that was punctuated by holes cast in the shape of the fixtures. Turning wall into ceiling, ceiling into floor, not to mention a third floor into what looks like a basement, the PS 1 project acquired its dizzying effect from a highly considered process of accumulation that accentuated the performative anchors of Seator's practice.

If all of the components of the PS1 installation seemed to be taking place concurrently—the temporality of which was reinforced by the lack of any

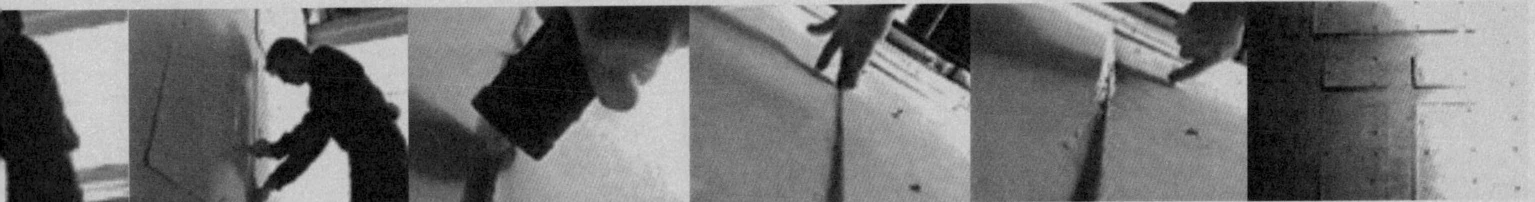

singular monument—then *Entrance*, 1994-95, at the Neuberger Museum of Art, emphatically concluded a procession though a space while maintaining its presence as the (ever-)present. It is a breakthrough work, surprisingly enough, in the actuating terms of its status not only as a solid, concrete (real) sculptural object, but also as a replica.[8] Positioned at the end of a path through a group exhibition entitled *Critical Distance: Between Art and Architecture*, what at first looks like a cold, brick cube is revealed to be a rebuilding of the museum entrance, condensed to the width of one pair of doors and placed on the axis of the actual entrance, which remains in view. Rotated ninety degrees, the doors (complete with their emergency "panic" bars) have re-appeared on the top of the cube, and the wooden ceiling grid that supports the lighting fixtures not only becomes the front of the piece, but also transforms the disorientated interior of the structure into a type of cage. Accompanied by a wallraising—titled *Moving Parts (Wallraising #7)*—that mapped Philip Johnson's crankshaft-inspired floor plan for the building, as well as discomforting museum benches that Seator altered by replacing their cushions with bricks matching those on the (effectively undercut) floor, *Entrance* returns to where it began in both time and space, drastically re-orienting not only the site of architecture, but also our (learned) sight of it.

Tipping *Entrance* completely over on its back insured that it would remain essentially sculptural, straightforward in its reference to minimalism. With *Cabinet*, 1995, Seator's decision to interrupt the tipping of the work itself—literally keeping a massive space in *suspense*—dramatically infused every aspect of both architecture and sculpture with the seemingly effortless manipulations usually reserved for photography and film. A virtual reconstruction of the dealer's private office held on edge at a thirty degree angle (complete with three openings/doorways on three of its sides), *Cabinet* (along with Seator's other "tipped" works discussed below) materialized the sort of oblique view one normally has when looking at that type of photograph in which the subject (the Eiffel Tower, for example) is deliberately or casually shot from a jarring angle, although the effect easily could be as simple (!) as that which occurs when holding *any* photograph askew. It honestly can be said that these works are ultimately felt in the gut, as was repeatedly acknowledged about *Cabinet*: "Though the human brain could correct the tilt, normalizing the structure so that it seemed straight, once your friends showed up grinning and waving at the other end, vertigo and panic struck, and you found yourself reaching for the Dramamine."[9]

Such nausea is a symptom provoked by the gap between the inside and outside of these works, a discrepancy between what first appears to be a monumental, even overwhelming exterior and a faithfully replicated, actual-size and human-scale interior. Moreover, this is a disjunction between the relative truths of sculpture and photography when it comes to our own bodies. Like *Cabinet*, both *N. Y. O. + B. (New York Office + Bathroom)*, 1996, and *B. D. O. (Breuer Director's Office)*, 1997, have been built in the most straightforward of manners with efficient construction techniques (including the replication of any design flaws in the original), their formal regularity and blankness perfectly in sync with our expectations learned from the terms of Tony Smith. Such integrity is re-interpreted on the inside, a representation that Seator relates to those embedded in the emulsion of a photograph, the material that contains the image that is supported by the "base" of the paper. To some extent, *B. D. O.* puts the finest point on this idea, not so much because it is a replica of the (powerful) Whitney Museum Director's office, but more because of the period specificity of its interior decoration (very Alfred Hitchcock).

With *N. Y. O. + B.*, the more dangerous examples of minimalism come to mind. Weighing more than 10,000 pounds, it is held in place by three cables, in a building that had once been heavily damaged by a fire. The presence of Seator's object mimics and challenges the modernist criteria for the ways in which a work of sculpture is meant to hit the ground as a formal object in space; yet again, on the inside (which isn't seen until after the viewer comes around from the other side) the piece is invested in a different set of criteria based in the conventions of realism. Its mediated reality is underscored by the inclusion of the bathroom with the office, the private space that is used for what Seator calls the "registration" (and maintenance) of the body. Such a recording is reinforced by the connecting wall between the two rooms that becomes a structurally agile bridge when isolated from the building's overall program, a path that leads to the surprise of truly "public" toilet. Seator would extend the terms of this connective approach in a project entitled *Facsimile*, 1996, at the Kunstraum Wien,

an installation that reconstructs the upstairs offices and the steps leading to them (which have been opened up to expose the storage in the "dead" space) in the main exhibition room below, putting a non-performative working environment on display within a facsimile of its normal space, which was transformed into a viewing space for the exhibition below. Suspended on temporary jacks as a sculpture, and released from the requirements of architecture, its slice-of-life recasts the terms of who and/or what is subject and/or object.

In "A Berlin Chronicle," Benjamin calls for a reconceptualization of *déjà vu*, a shift from sight to sound: "Accordingly, if we are not mistaken, the shock with which moments enter consciousness as if already lived usually strike us in the form of a sound. It is a word, tapping, or a rustling that is endowed with the magic power to transport us into the cool tomb of long ago, from the vault of which the present seems to return only as an echo."[10] It is clear that Benjamin reached his reappraisal with his mind (not to mention his body) on the street, as a site where the appearance of daily activity can usually be interpreted, understood, and remembered by taking advantage of the ideological suggestiveness of sound. Such a critical re-orientation is accomplished in Seator's most ambitious project to date, one made all the more poignant by its ultimate disappearance. Using more than 250 tons of concrete, gravel, asphalt, wood, glass, and steel, *Approach*, 1997, faithfully reproduced the façade of San Francisco's Capp Street Project along with the stretch of Second Street in front of it (including the sidewalk, street lights, etc.), installing everything as a literal *overlay* inside the exhibition space. Unlike most scrupulous representations—particularly Dutch landscape painting, which Seator reminded me was often commissioned by landowners as legal documents, maps of ownership often placed next to the view they held—it is possible to stand inside

Seator's and stare back at its source, performing a highly self-conscious form of *flânerie* that pushes daily activity to the extreme, concretizing it, and surely making us hyper-aware of the discourse we participate in while walking the real street. In addition, it should be understood that the material and conceptual status of *Approach* as an overlay which makes no attempt to disguise the existing structure of the gallery (much of which remains empty behind the work) makes the work neither theme park nor *trompe l'œil*.[11] This point is re-emphasized in *within the lines of the studs*, 1997, a cinematic return to a scene just completed: after we've entered a gallery (and not the coin shop next door), we go up some stairs, down a corridor and make a right turn right back where we started, *almost*. The object of our return is a strangely self-contained sculpture that we can either enter or walk around.[12]

It is a cliché to say that no one walks in Los Angeles, but millions of people do. With *Three*, Seator performs a cut and paste on long tracking shots that move from a blank desert area closest to L.A., or a check-cashing store on Sunset Boulevard in Echo Park, to a temporary resting place at a Beverly Hills gallery. In a reversal of the typical conditions of entertainment, which asks for (and usually receives) our passivity, he presents a single-frame panoramic photograph as a still image that the viewer must move in front of in order to take it all in. With a replication of a check cashing store adding a disjunctive address—not to mention enterprise—to the street (by the way, Benjamin would notice that it's one-way), Seator not only literalizes and collides those boundaries that are kept in place by hugely disproportionate distributions of wealth, but also demands (as has been the case in all of his work) that we continue to pay attention to the folds in any machine—desiring or not. By doing this, he and his desiring-machines are very far along in their non-fascist lives.

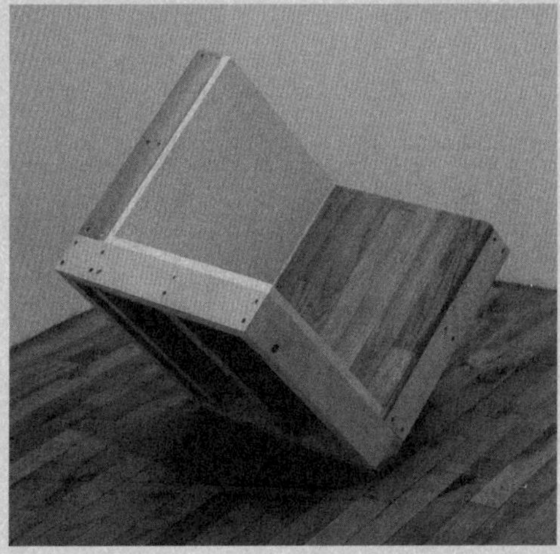

Universal Corner
1992
wood, sheetrock, screws, polyurethane, wall paint
19" x 19" x 19"

NOTES

[1] Michel Foucault, "Preface," in Gilles Deleuze and Félix Guattari, *Anti-Oedipus: Capitalism and Schizophrenia* (Minneapolis: University of Minnesota Press, 1983), xiv.

[2] Walter Benjamin, "A Berlin Chronicle," in *Reflections* (New York: Schocken Books, 1978), 6.

[3] Deleuze and Guattari, 1.

[4] See Anna C. Chave, "Minimalism and The Rhetoric of Power," *Arts Magazine* 64 (January 1990), 44-63. The questions Chave asks in her ground-breaking text are crucial to an understanding of the conflicting complexities of minimalism; to cite only one example: "... how are to understand [minimalism's] cool displays of power in relation to a society that was experiencing a violent ambivalence toward authority, a society where many were looking for the means of transforming power relations?" (p. 44)

[5] All quotations and comments from the artist are taken from conversations on May 13 and 15, 1999.

[6] Attentive to both the commodification and the leveling of identity politics and difference as effective strategies to get rid of them, in conversation Seator spoke with tremendous insight about how he symbolically perceived a large amount of work and exhibitions from the early 1990s as a series of "curio cabinets" in which accumulations of difference were being "swept into one pile."

[7] See Tim Rollins, "Felix Gonzalez-Torres was interviewed by Tim Rollins at his New York apartment on April 16 and June 12, 1993," in *Felix Gonzalez-Torres* (Los Angeles: Art Resources Transfer, 1993), 20.

[8] Beginning with the exhibition of *Entrance* in January 1995, Seator's re-introduction of the suggestive conditions of the full-blown replica into contemporary art discourse has had a certain impact on the work of other artists, most strikingly Rirkrit Tiravanija's *Untitled (Play Time)*, 1997—a one-half scale fabrication of Philip Johnson's *Glass House* that was installed in MoMA's sculpture garden and used for children's art classes.

[9] Lisa Anne Auerbach, "Glen Seator, Burnett Miller Gallery," *Artforum* 34 (March 1996), 105-106.

[10] Benjamin, 59.

[11] Seator's desire to let the seams show in theory and practice reminds me most of the work of Larry Johnson. See my recent text, "Larry Johnson: we were never being boring," *art/text*, no. 64 (February-April 1999), 52-57, from which the following passage could also be said about Seator's work: "It would not be misleading to suggest that the space of the physical gaps and seams of [Johnson's] 1994 and 1995 works has turned a quarter-revolution into the dimensional space of [the] new photographs themselves, a space which now approximates that found between us and the work in the first place, a reconfiguring of the relationship between *faktura* and factography, a productive negotiation between the physical construction of the "icon" and the jarring juxtapositions of photomontage." (pp. 56-57)

[12] Given the text on a plaque attached to the building's façade—"HIGHWAYS ACT 1959 / THIS FORECOURT WITHIN THE LINE OF THE STUDS IS PRIVATE PROPERTY AND NO PUBLIC RIGHTS EXIST THEREOVER"—David Barrett's "boilerplate" review of Seator's London exhibition smartly hits its target. (The first line: "Duke Street is expensive.") See David Barrett, "Glen Seator," *Art Monthly*, no. 209 (September 1997). Barrett's read could easily be applied to a subsequent work of Seator's not discussed here, *Sculpture with French Desk and Receptionist*, 1998, which replicated the glass façade and front room of the Mary Boone Gallery in Soho, placing it like a hallucinatory memory (good or bad, depending on your point of view) in her new 57th Street space.

Terry R. Myers is a critic and curator currently based in Los Angeles. A contributing editor to *art/text*, *Blocnotes*, and *New Art Examiner*, he is Editor of a book on painting from 1945-2000, forthcoming from Phaidon Press Limited.

SELECTED PROJECTS

Untitled (Auditorium Installation)
1993
existing light fixtures and bulbs, steel chain, double sided tape, sweeping compound,
daily sweeping accumulations and earth
dimensions variable
PS1 Museum, The Institute for Contemporary Art, New York

The existing light fixtures and bulbs are extended with chain matching the original.
The daily sweeping of the room is organized around the lowered lighting grid.

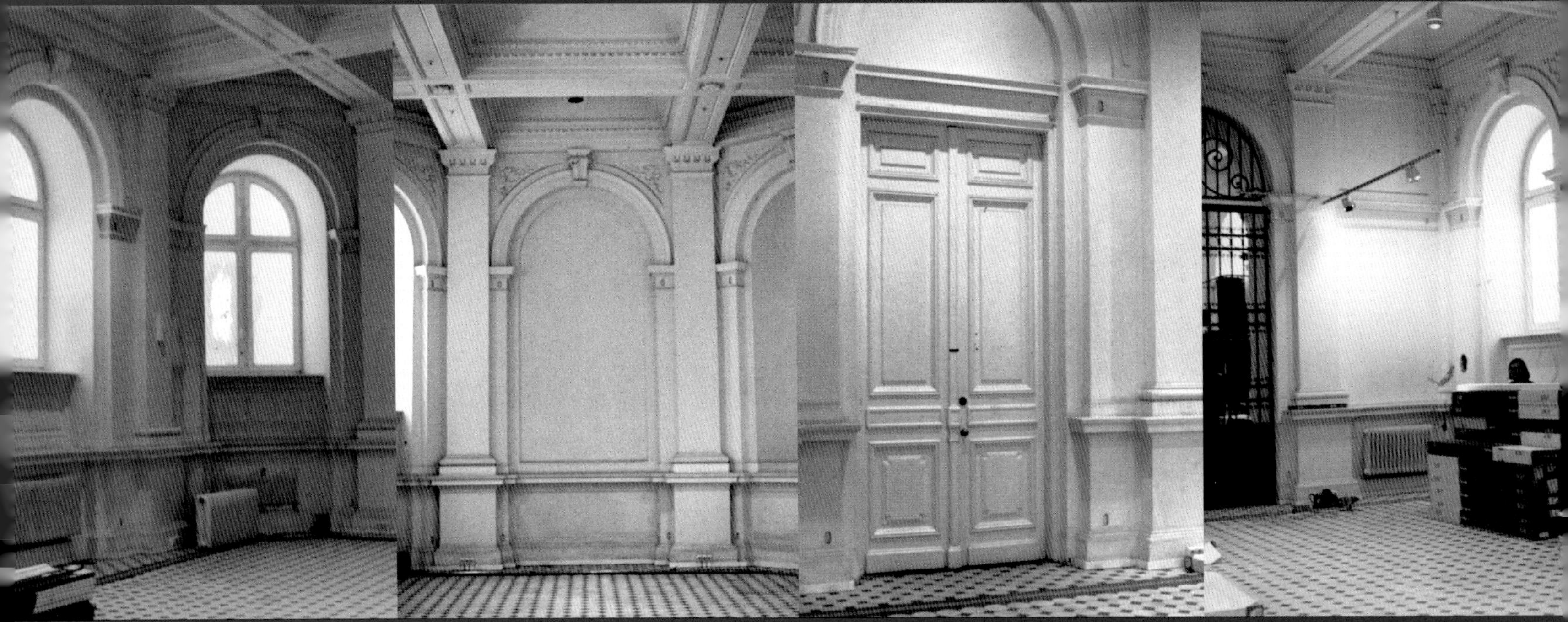

existing conditions at The National Gallery of Contemporary Art (Zaçheta), Warsaw

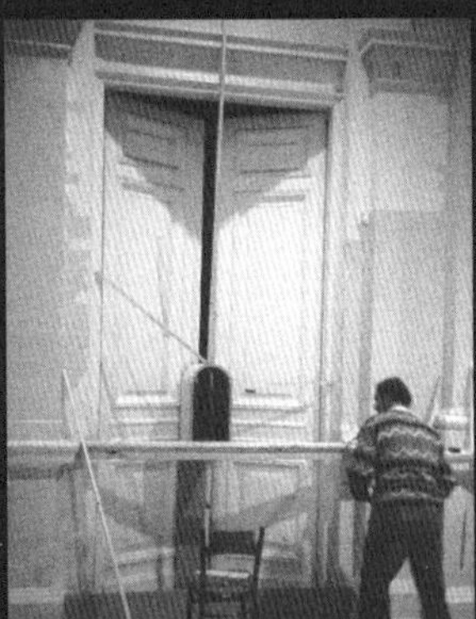

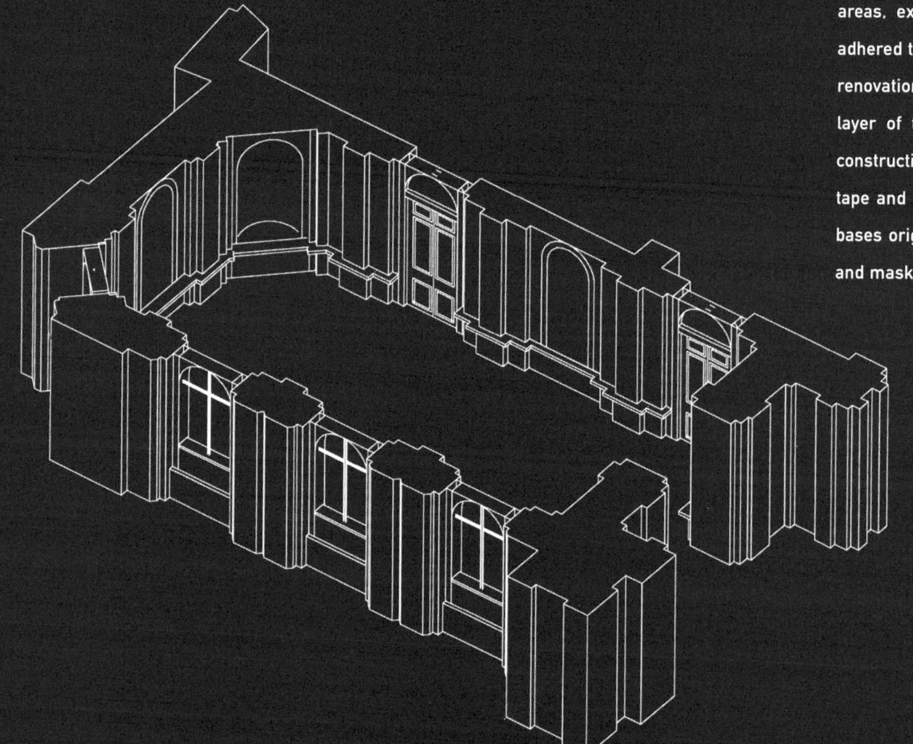

The room is rebuilt from the ground up: tape is stretched in continuous horizontal courses over the walls and the voids within the arches, creating a masked plane in front of the windows, blind windows, doors and sculpture niches. The blind window serves as the prototype for the reconstruction of the area within each arch: horizontal moldings are mimicked with the application of tape over thin strips of wood. In other areas, existing moldings and other details remain articulated under the tightly adhered tape. In the doorway between the gallery and an area of the building under renovation, a small arched portal is constructed: the doors are opened, and the thin layer of tape becomes the only barrier separating the gallery from the heavy construction beyond. Throughout the course of the day, sunlight passes through the tape and the walls appear to change from transparent to solid. Like the sculpture bases originally used here, the objects on the floor — constructed of strips of wood and masking tape — reflects the form of the room's plinths.

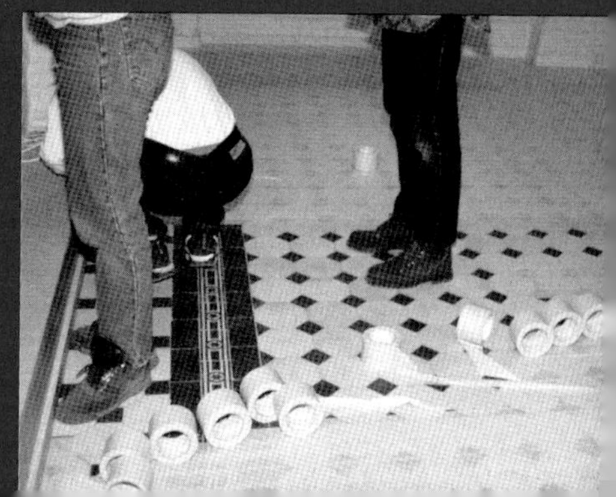

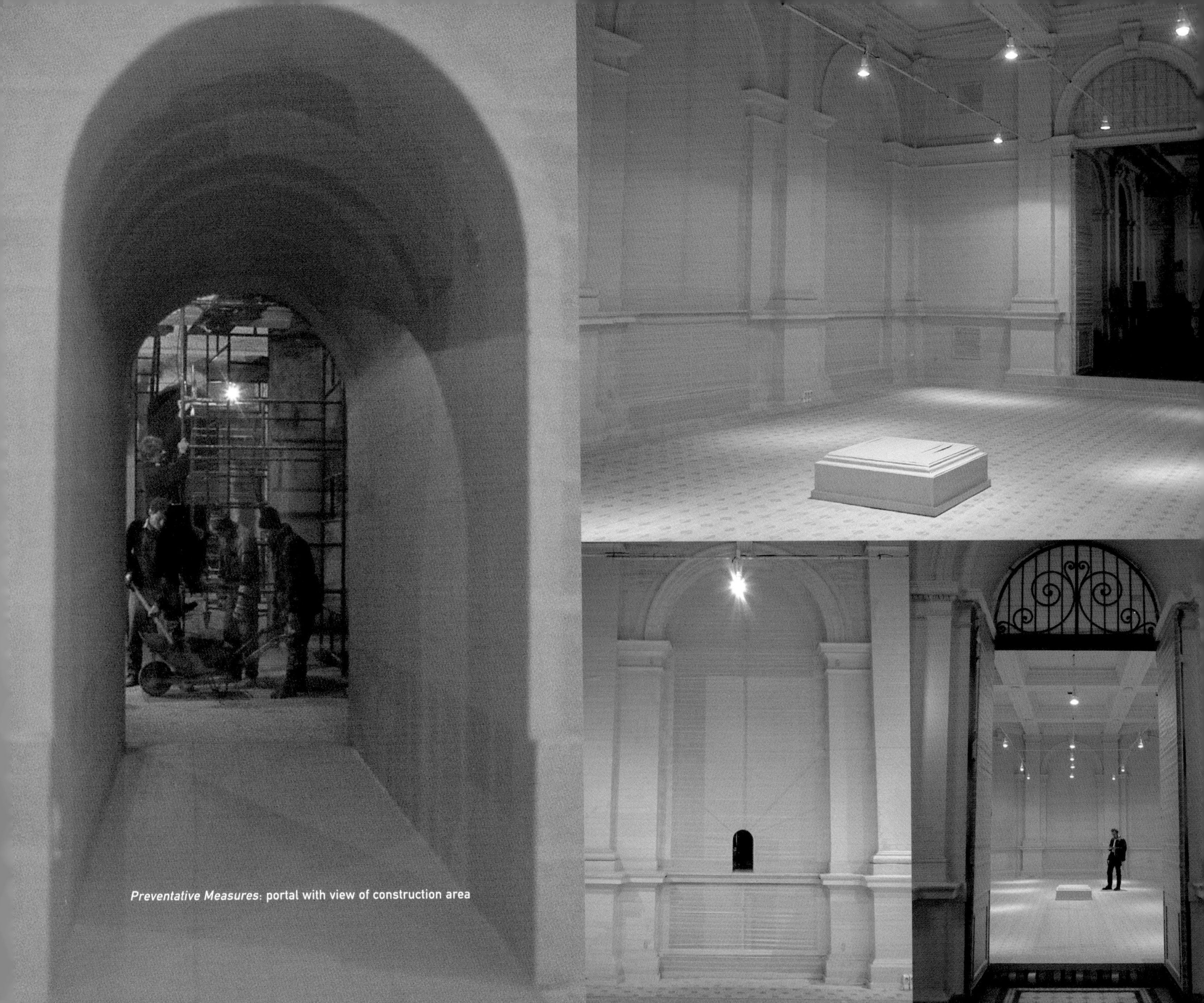

Preventative Measures: portal with view of construction area

Entrance

1994-95

brick, mortar, steel, glass doors, wood

8' x 8' x 8'

Neuberger Museum of Art, Purchase, New York

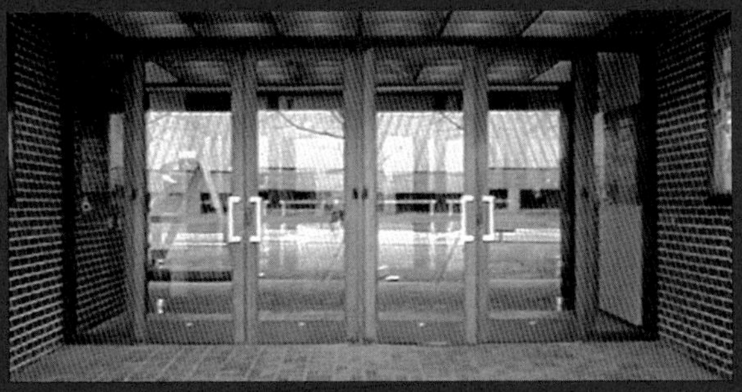

Moving Parts (Wallraising #7)

1990-95

14' x 40'

incised and raised existing sheetrock, raised screws

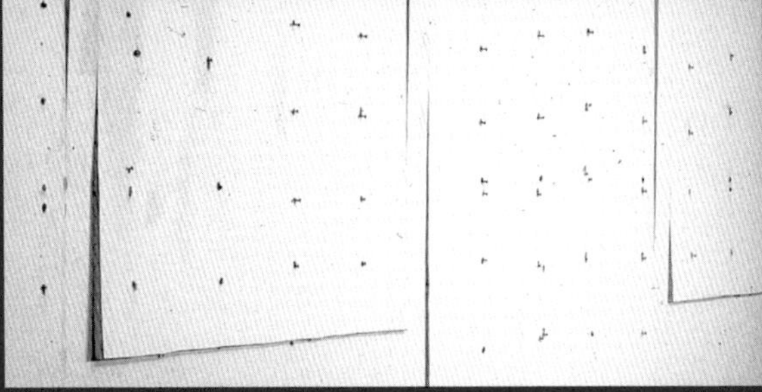

Untitled (altered benches)

1994-95

20" x 24" x 72"

chromium-plated steel bench frames, brick, mortar

Entrance is a reconstruction of the entryway of the Philip Johnson designed building. Placed on its side on the axis of the actual entrance, the work is visible upon
entering the museum. The materials are identical to those originally used in the
building.

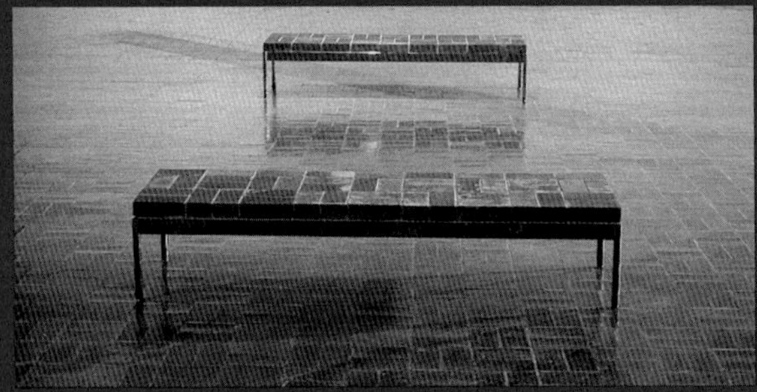

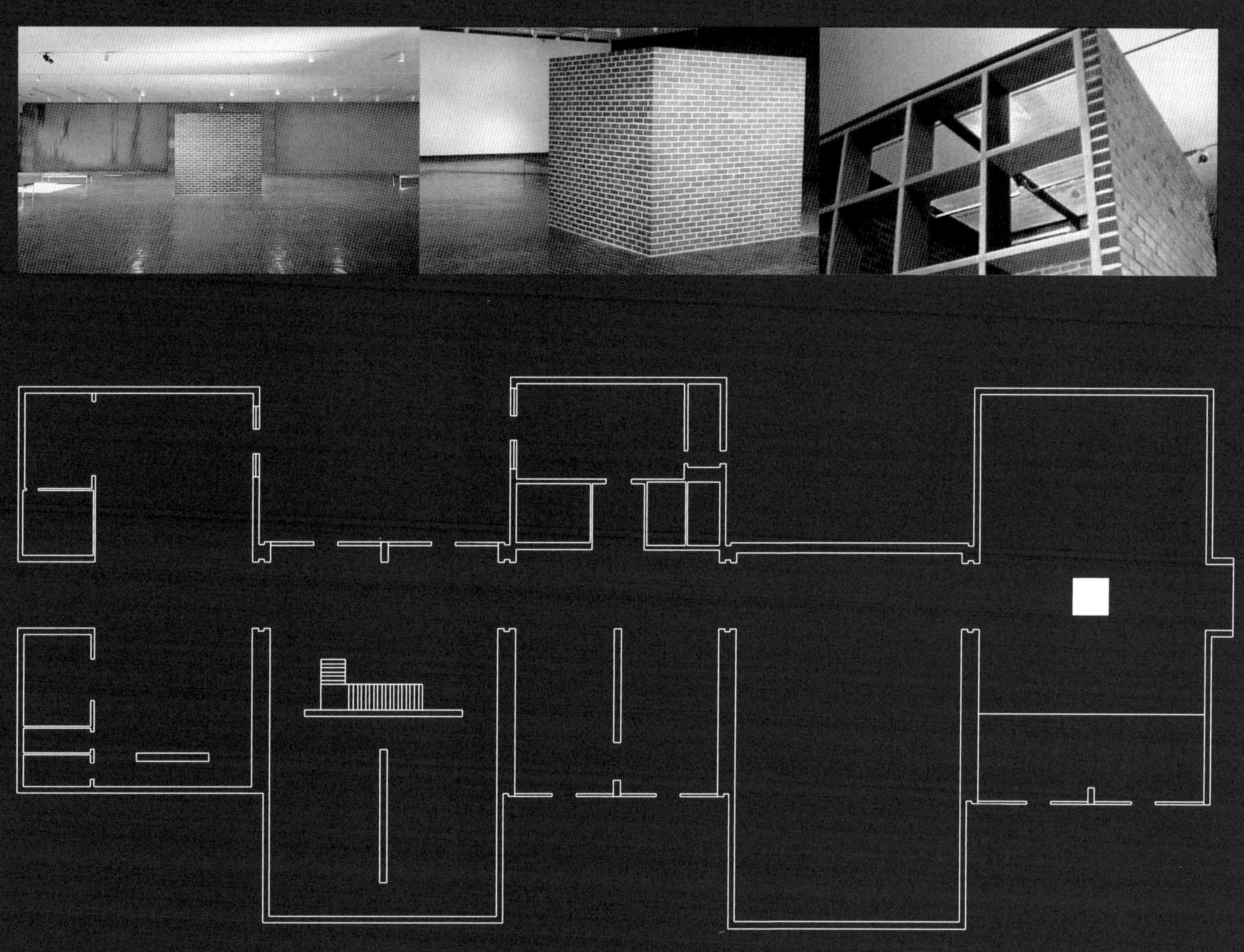

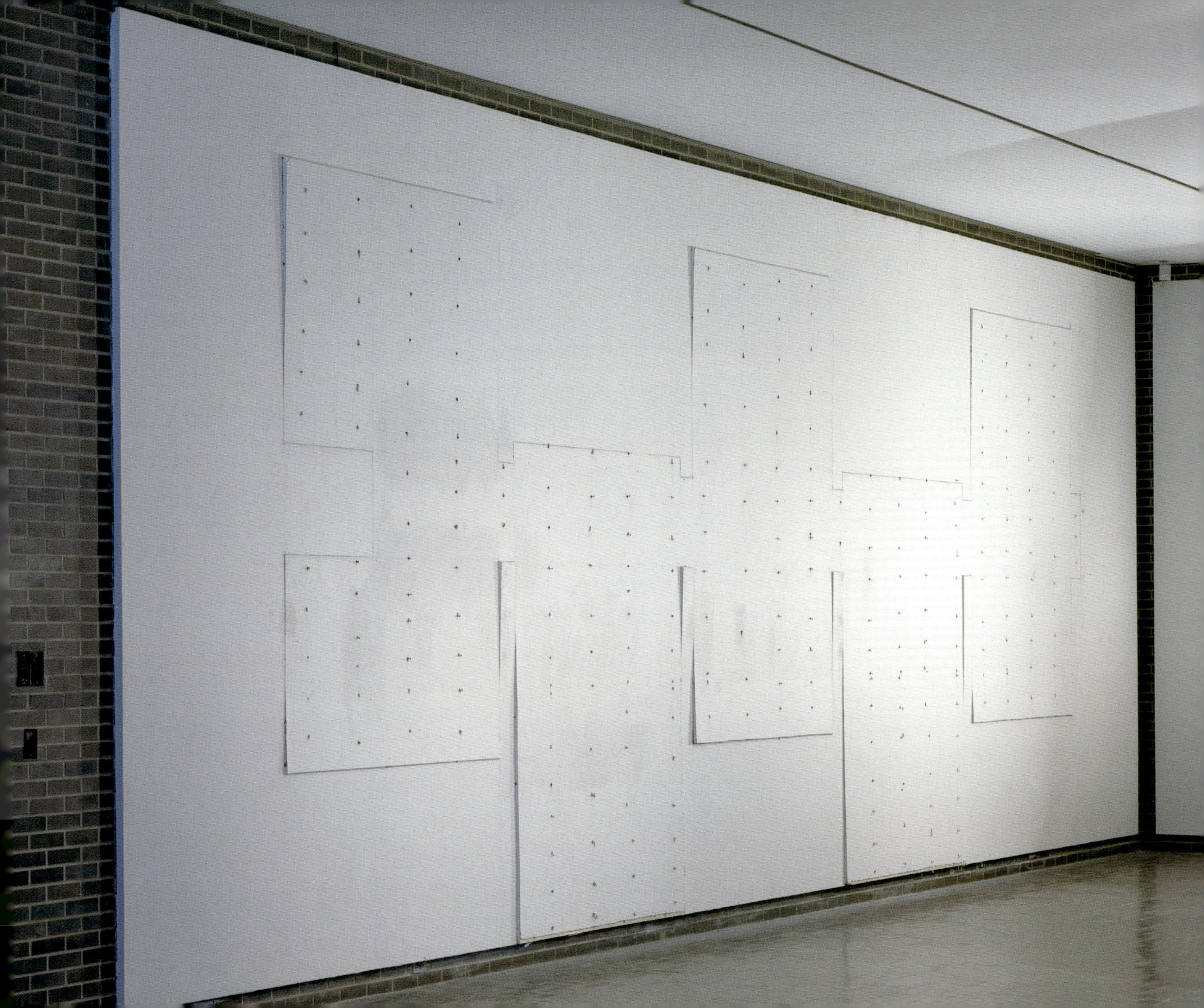

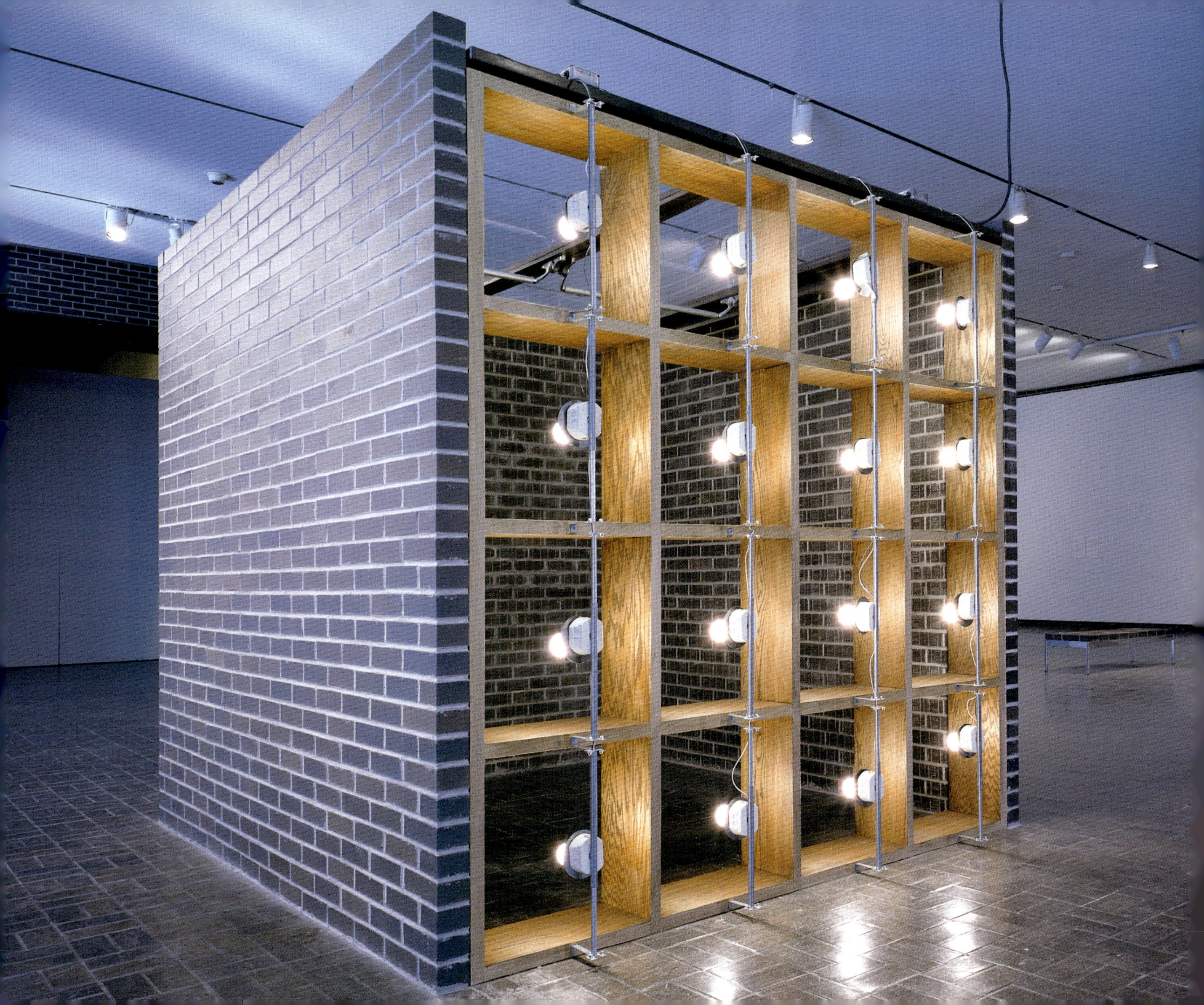

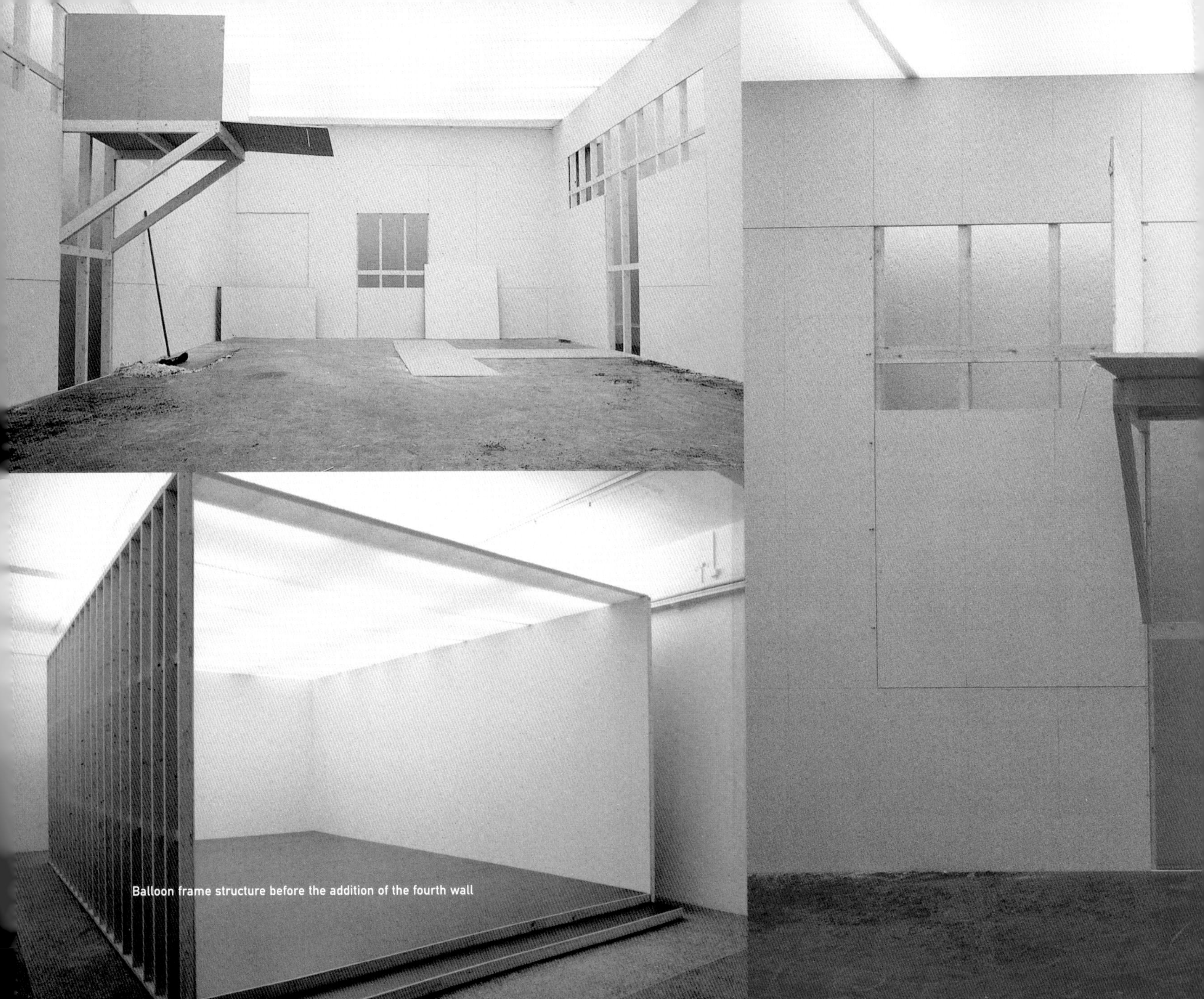
Balloon frame structure before the addition of the fourth wall

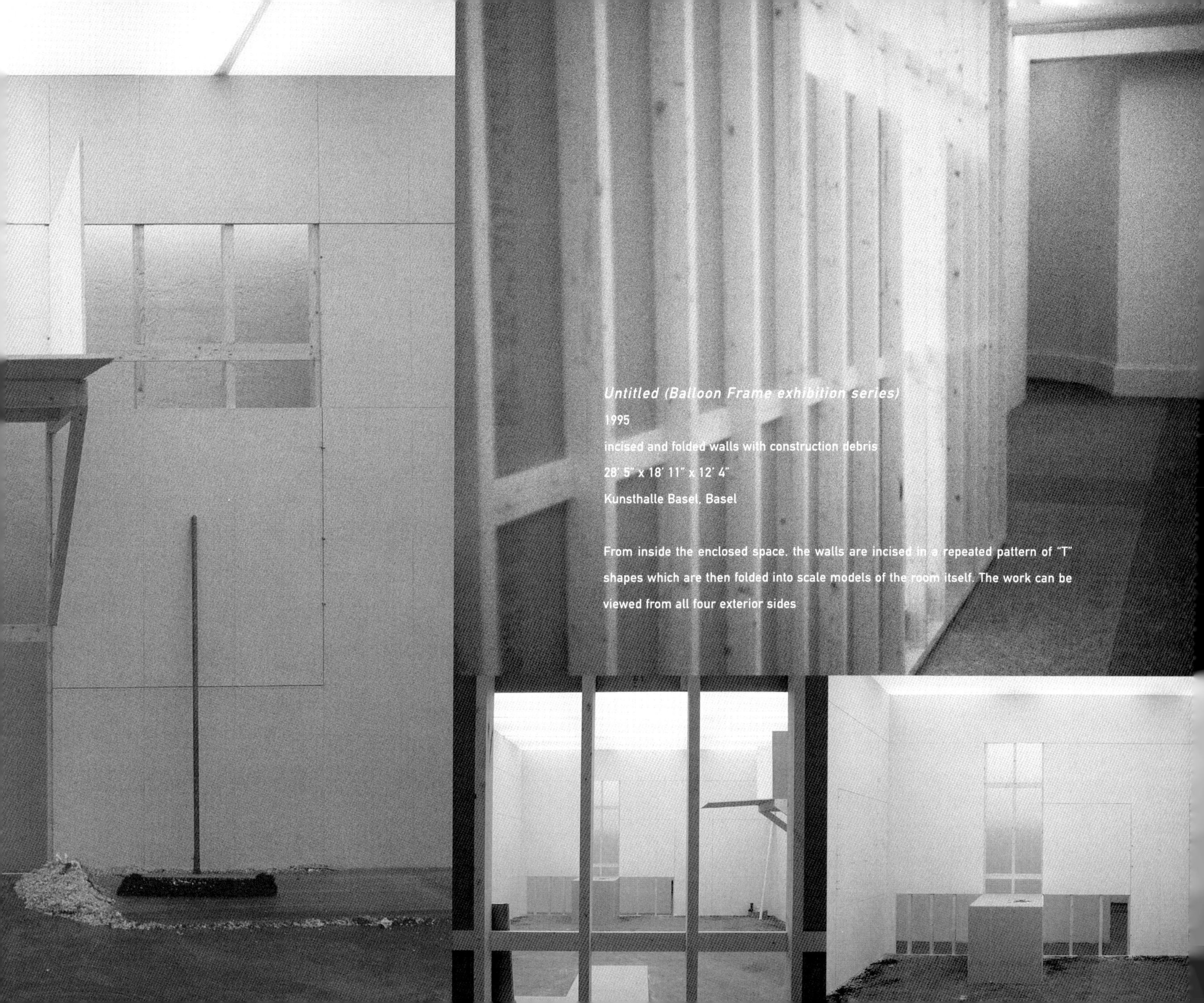

Untitled (Balloon Frame exhibition series)
1995
incised and folded walls with construction debris
28' 5" x 18' 11" x 12' 4"
Kunsthalle Basel, Basel

From inside the enclosed space, the walls are incised in a repeated pattern of "T" shapes which are then folded into scale models of the room itself. The work can be viewed from all four exterior sides

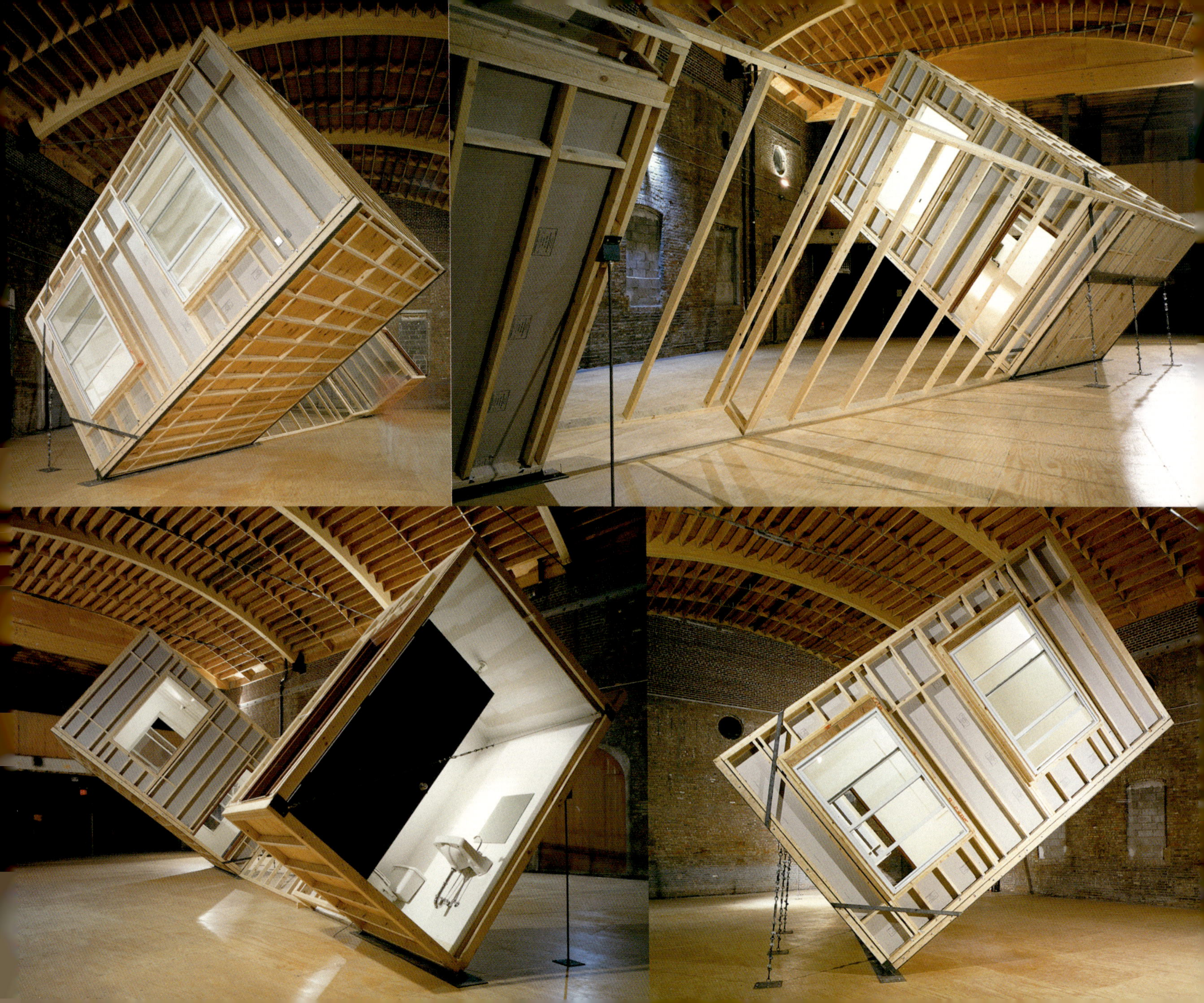

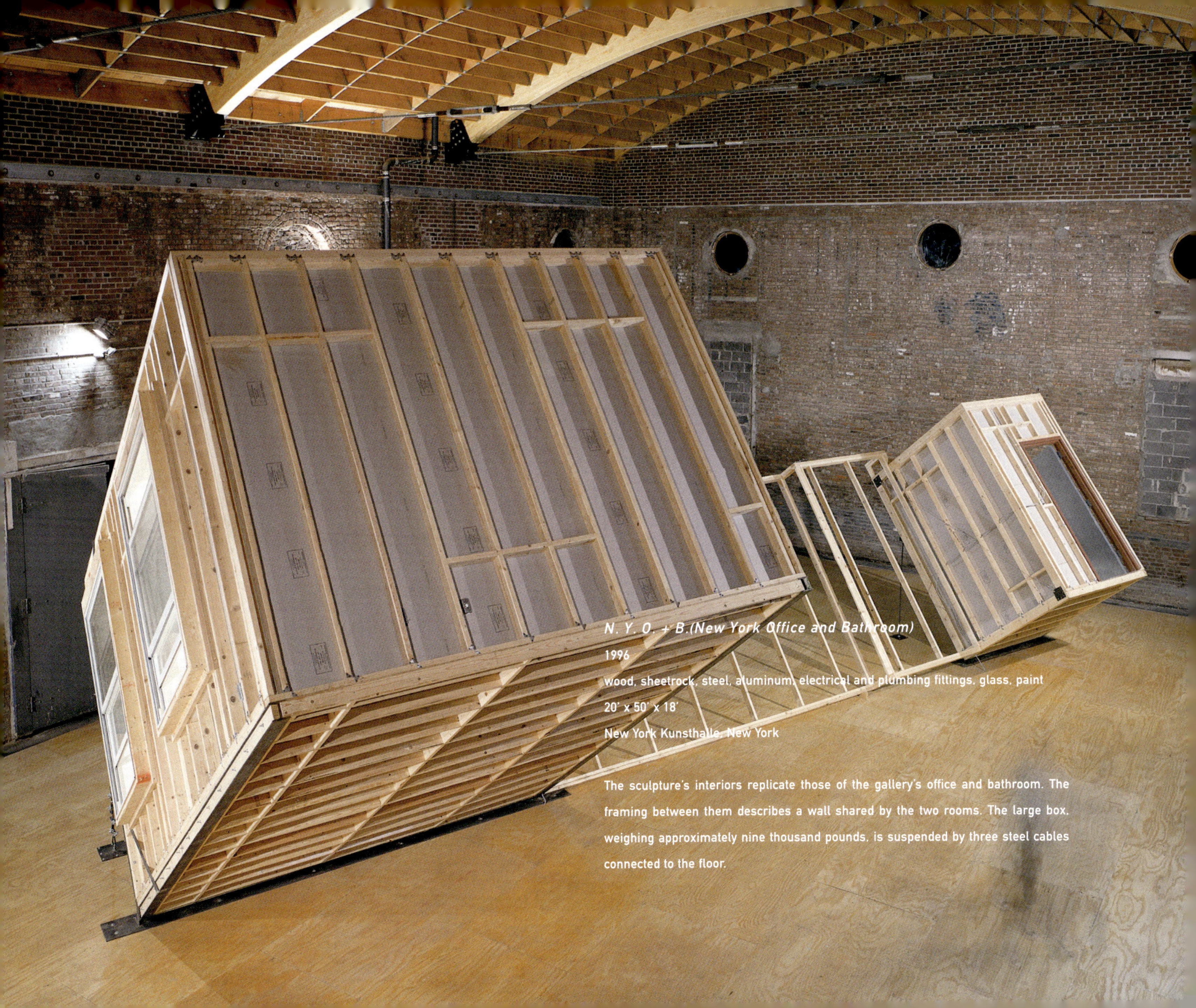

N. Y. O. + B.(New York Office and Bathroom)
1996
wood, sheetrock, steel, aluminum, electrical and plumbing fittings, glass, paint
20' x 50' x 18'
New York Kunsthalle, New York

The sculpture's interiors replicate those of the gallery's office and bathroom. The framing between them describes a wall shared by the two rooms. The large box, weighing approximately nine thousand pounds, is suspended by three steel cables connected to the floor.

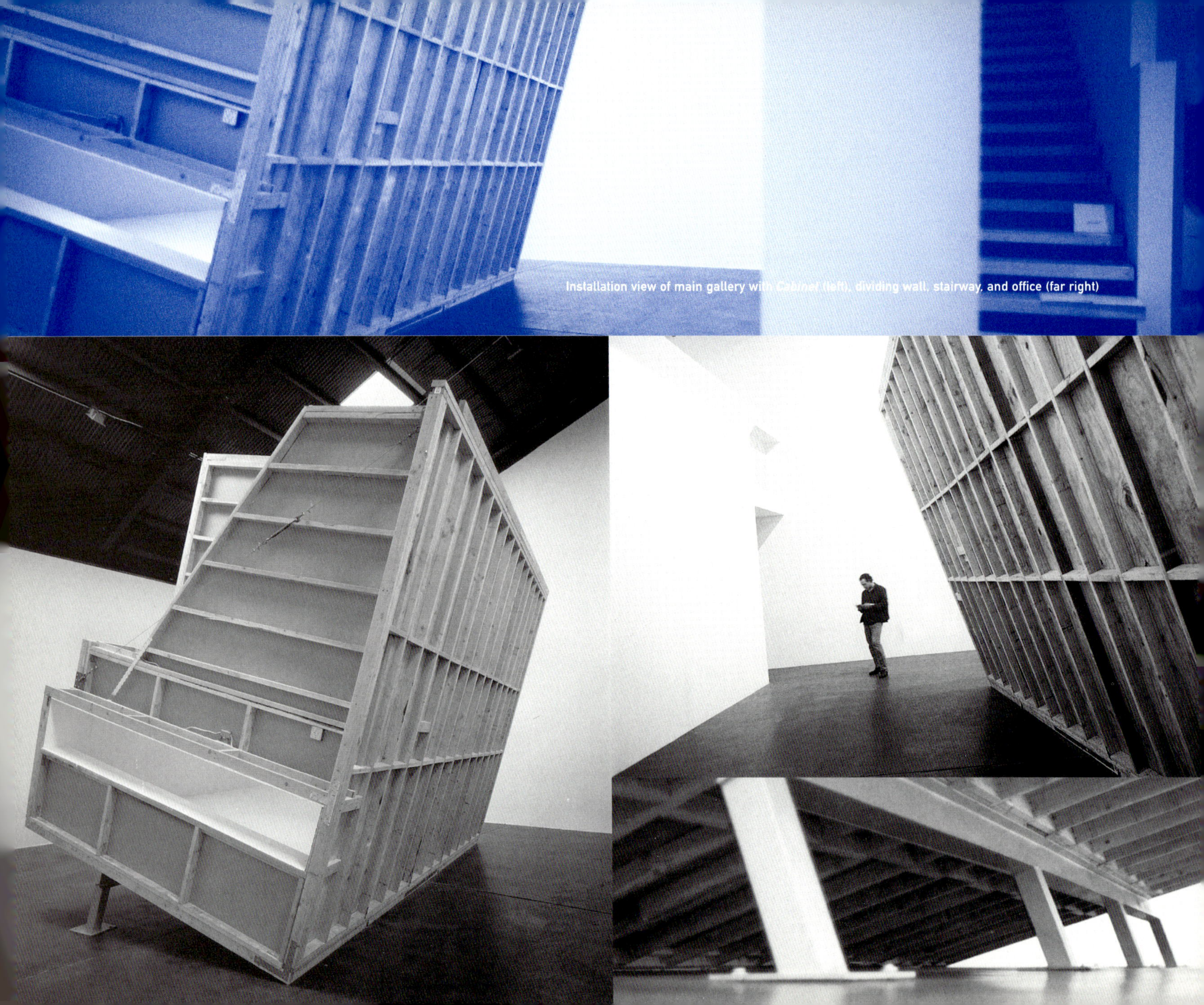

Installation view of main gallery with *Cabinet* (left), dividing wall, stairway, and office (far right)

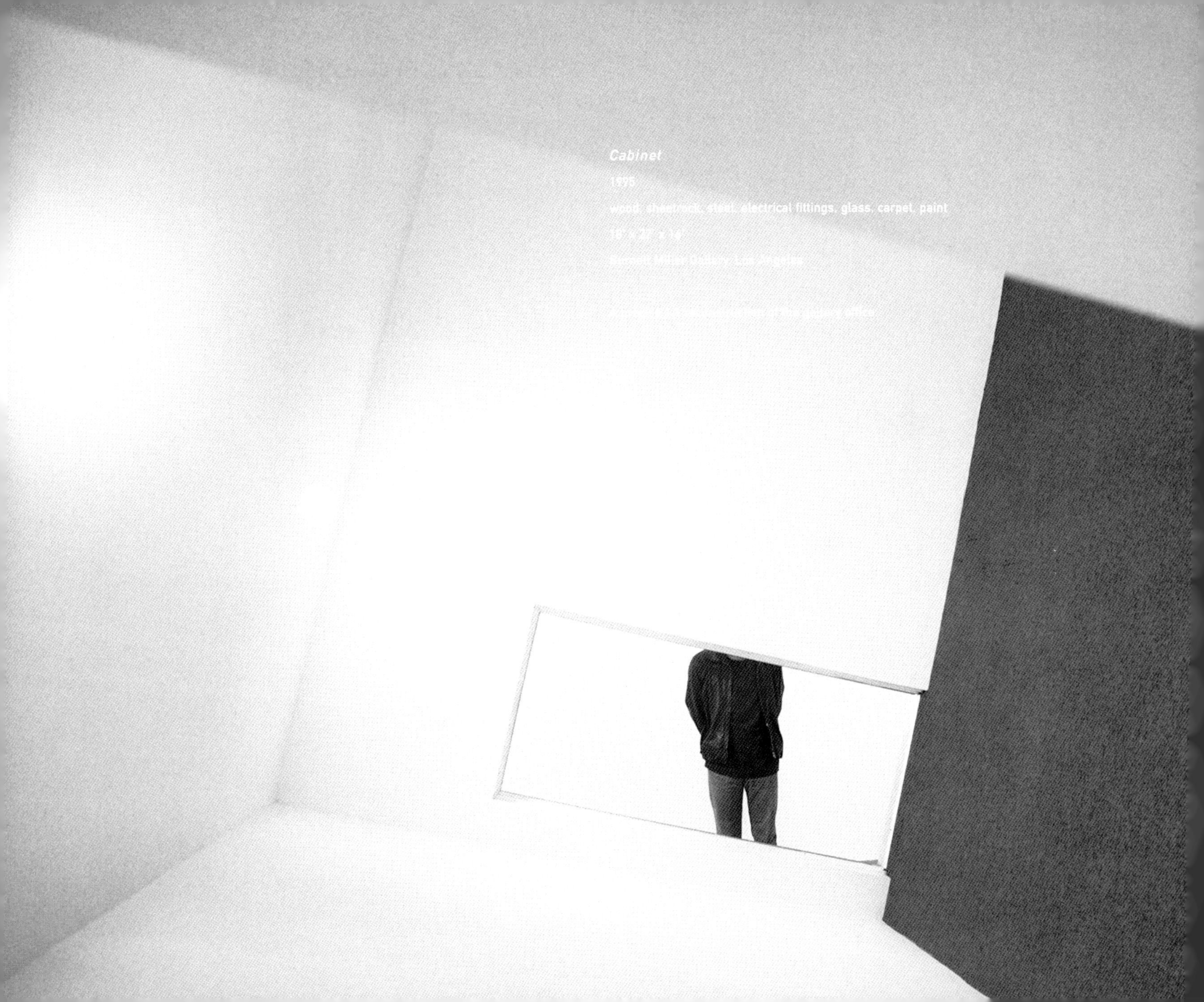

Cabinet
1995
wood, sheetrock, steel, electrical fittings, glass, carpet, paint
15' x 27' x 14'
Burnett Miller Gallery, Los Angeles

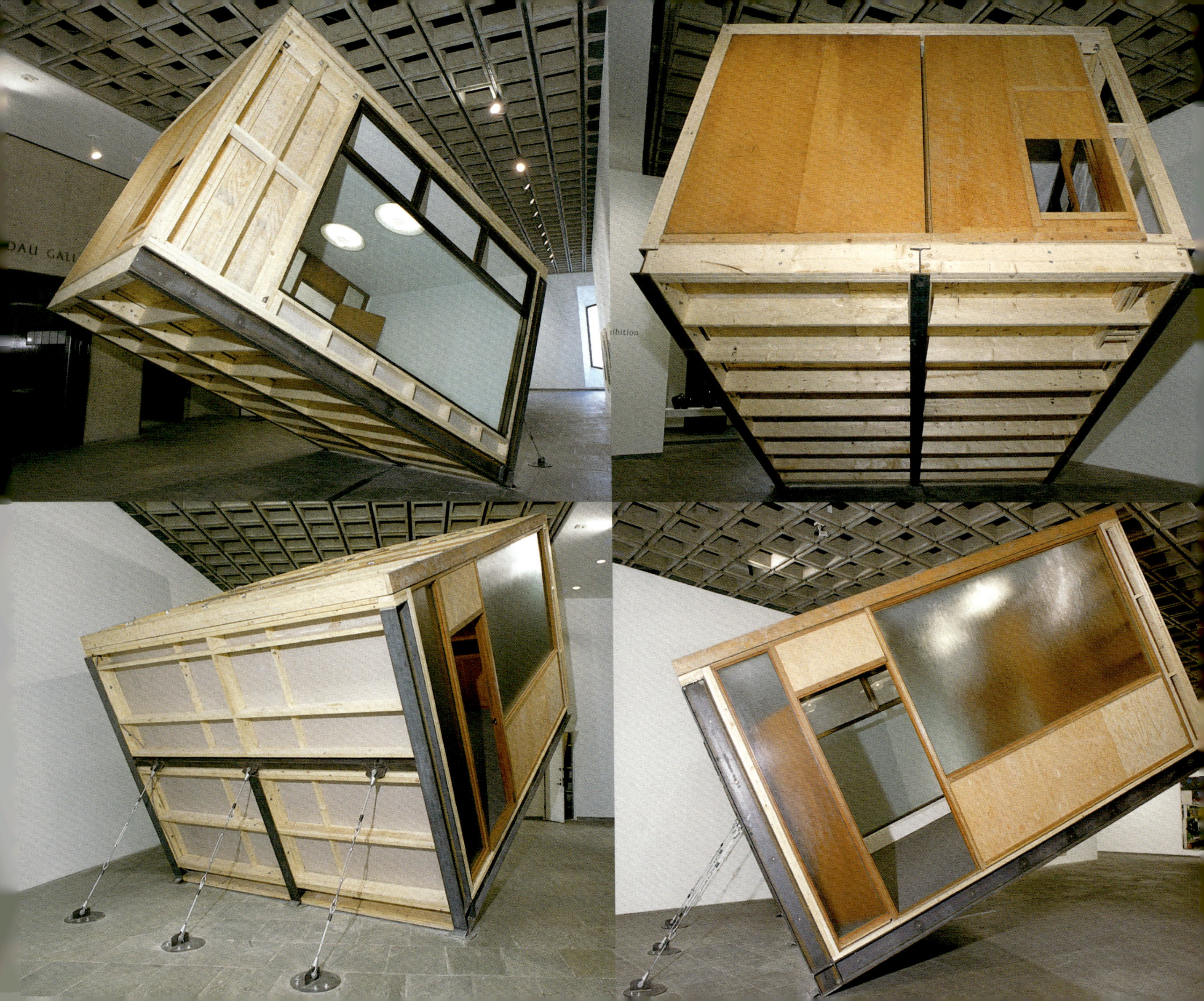

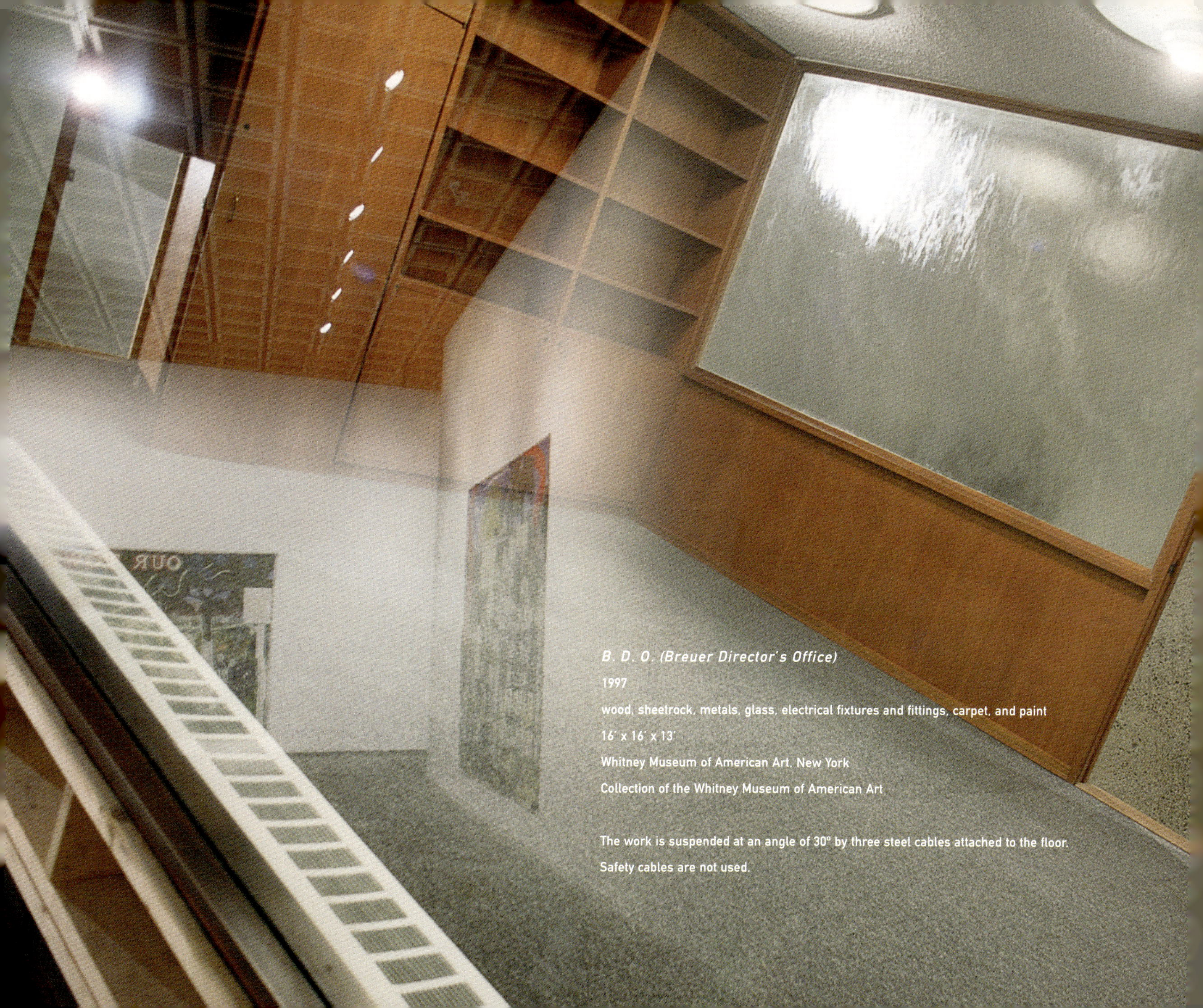

B. D. O. (Breuer Director's Office)
1997
wood, sheetrock, metals, glass, electrical fixtures and fittings, carpet, and paint
16' x 16' x 13'
Whitney Museum of American Art, New York
Collection of the Whitney Museum of American Art

The work is suspended at an angle of 30° by three steel cables attached to the floor.
Safety cables are not used.

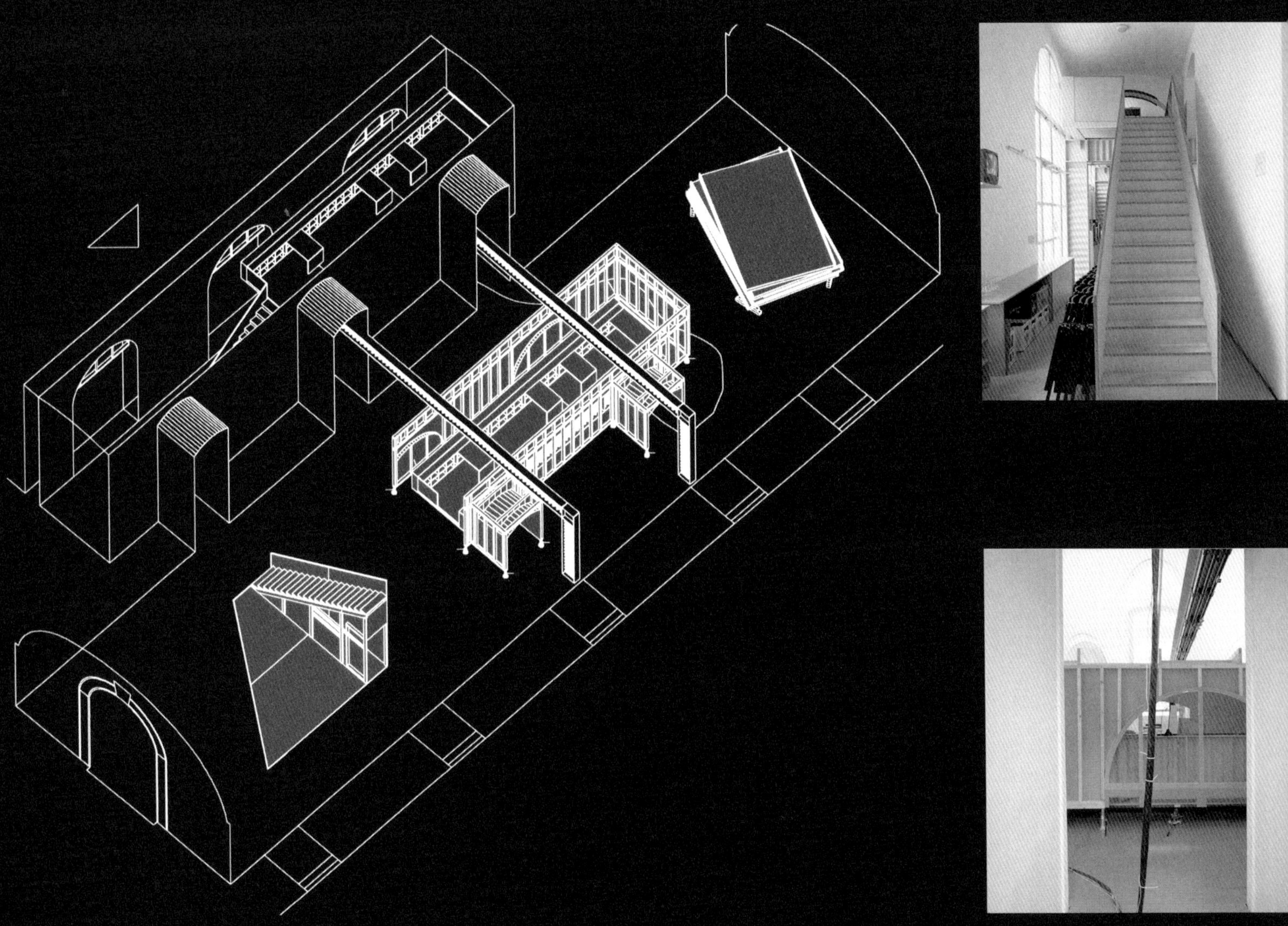

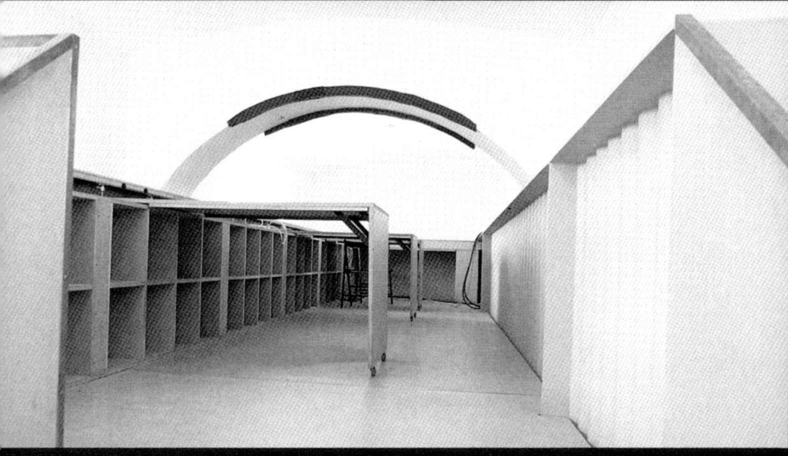

Stairway to emptied (original) office

Three views from reception area into main gallery

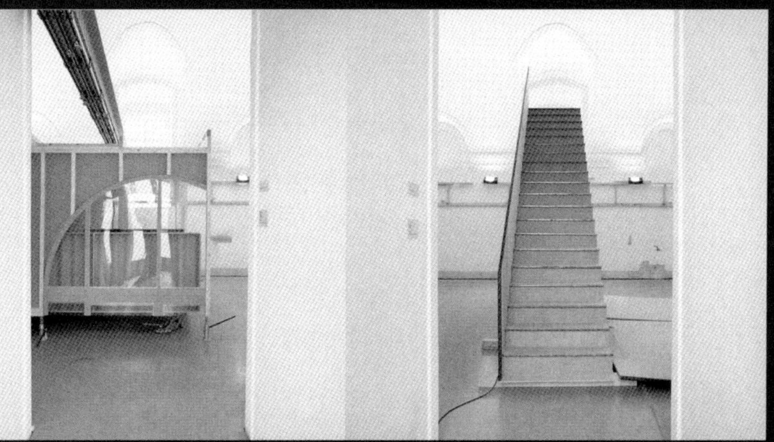

Facsimile

1995-96

wood, plexi-glass, resin, sheetrock, hydraulic jacks, fittings, contents of emptied office (supplies, furniture, staff) and contents of emptied supply closet

office sculpture: 9' x 30' x 12', stairway/closet sculpture: 14' x 18' x 3'

Kunstraum Wien, Vienna

This Fischer von Erlach building was adapted for use as an exhibition space with the addition of sliding gallery walls and the construction of an office on an I-beam bridge overlooking the gallery. The sliding walls are removed and stacked, and the office and stairway with maintenance closet are reconstructed and presented as sculptures in the main gallery. The contents of the office and the closet — including staff — are relocated and become part of the objects on display. The daily work is conducted in the main gallery over the three month run of the exhibition. At the foot of the original stairway a sign is installed inviting visitors to enter the emptied office space — with a view over the gallery and sculptures.

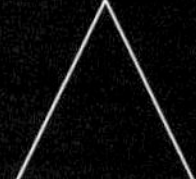

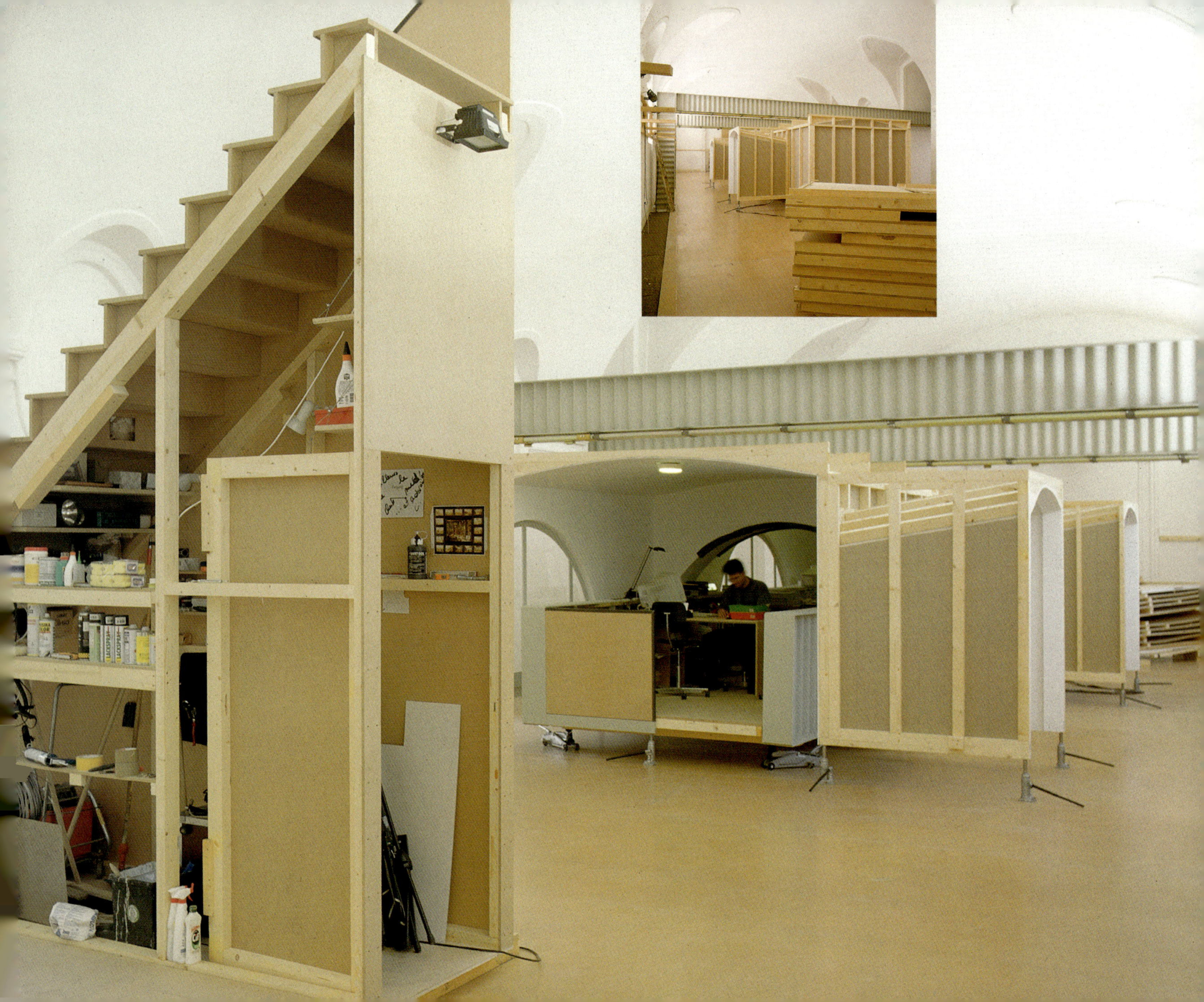

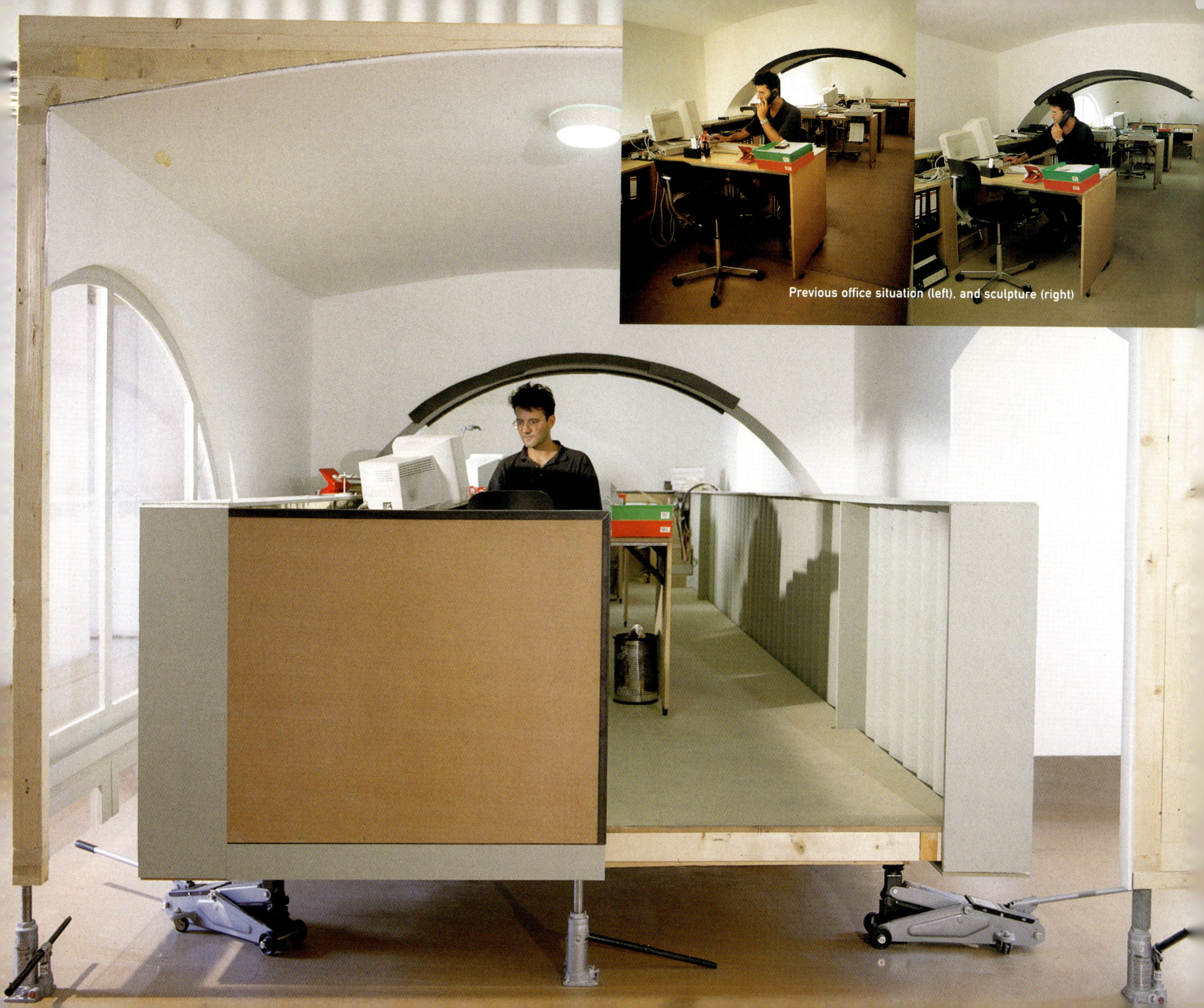

Previous office situation (left), and sculpture (right)

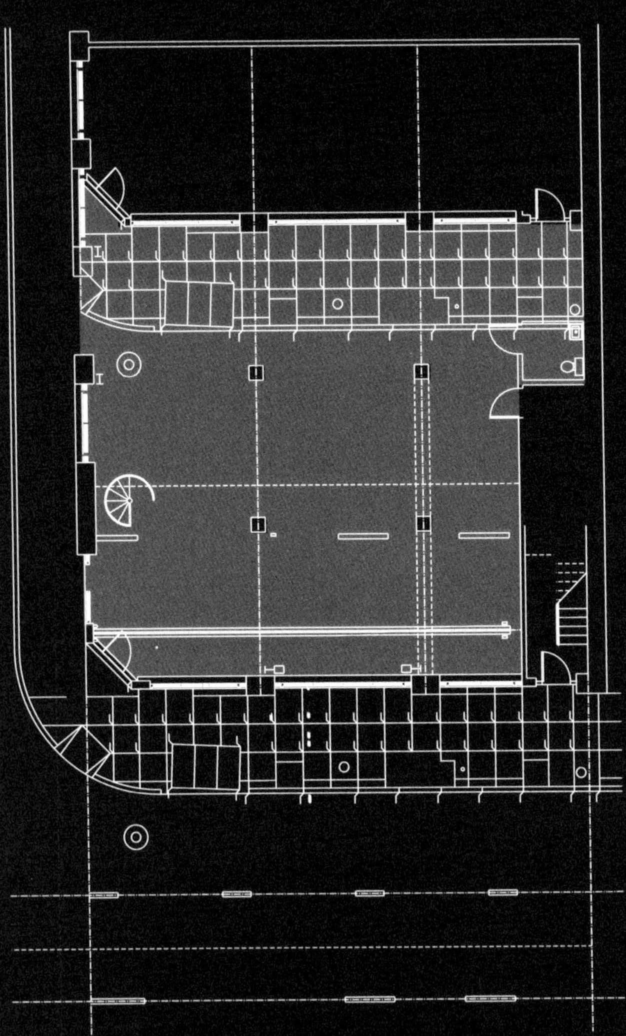

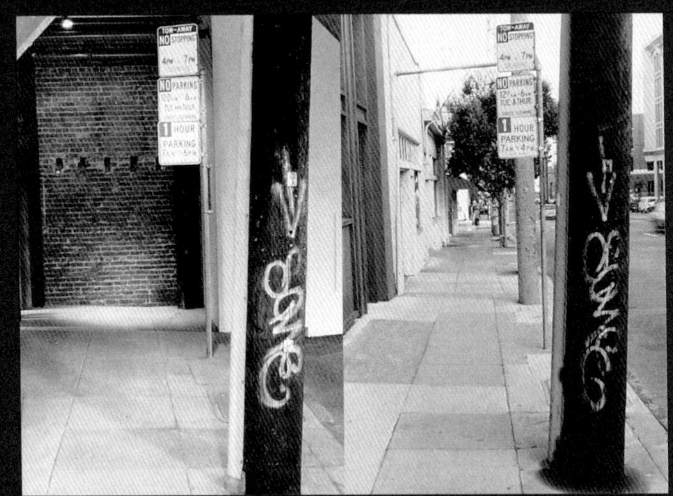

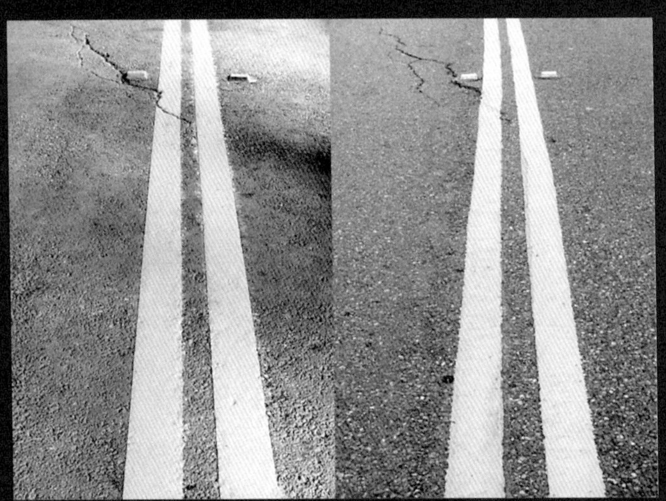

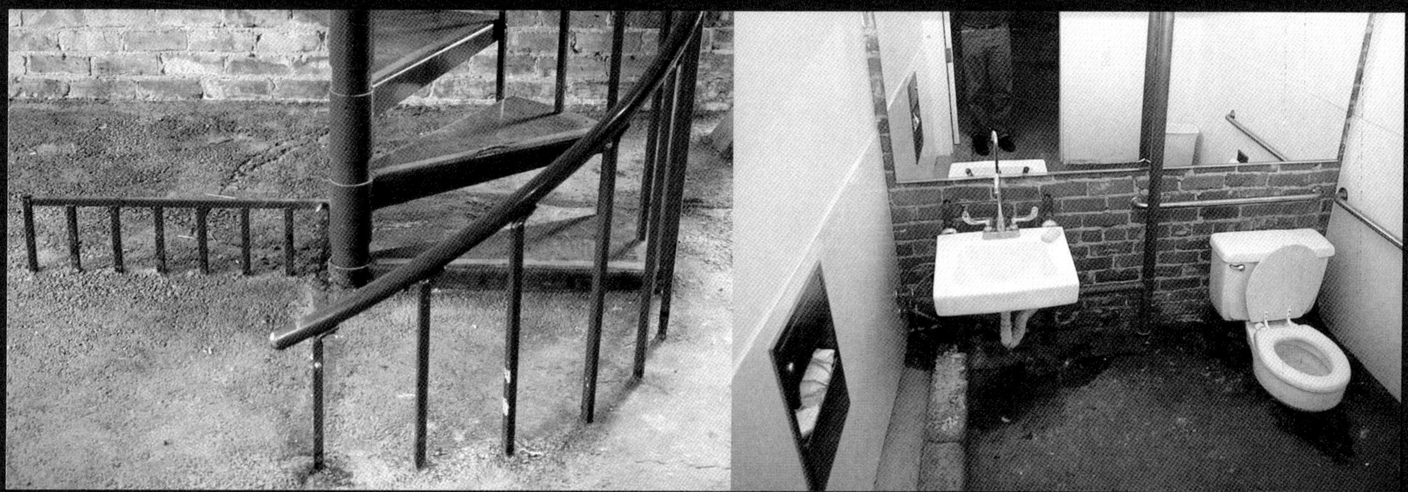

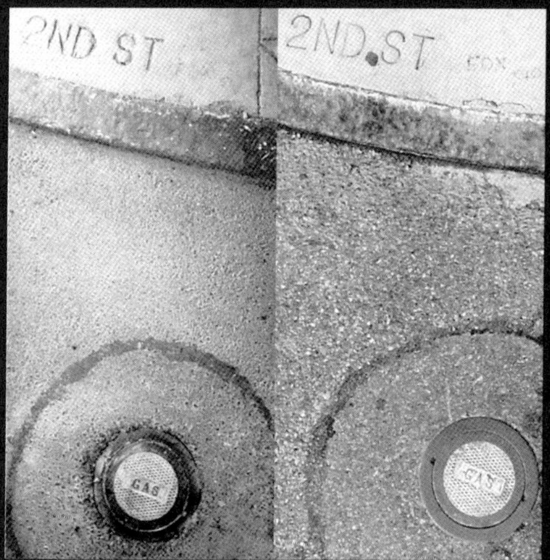

Approach
1997
gravel fill, sand fill, asphalt, concrete, wood, glass, metals, electrical fixtures, and
thermal striping
56' x 80' x 16'
Capp Street Project, San Francisco

Using approximately 250 tons of materials, the façade and section of sidewalk and
street fronting Capp Street Project is rebuilt inside the gallery. With the use of the
same materials as the actual exterior components, the various grades and details of
street and sidewalk are precisely reproduced. The replicated street terrain rises as
much as 40 inches above the existing gallery floor.

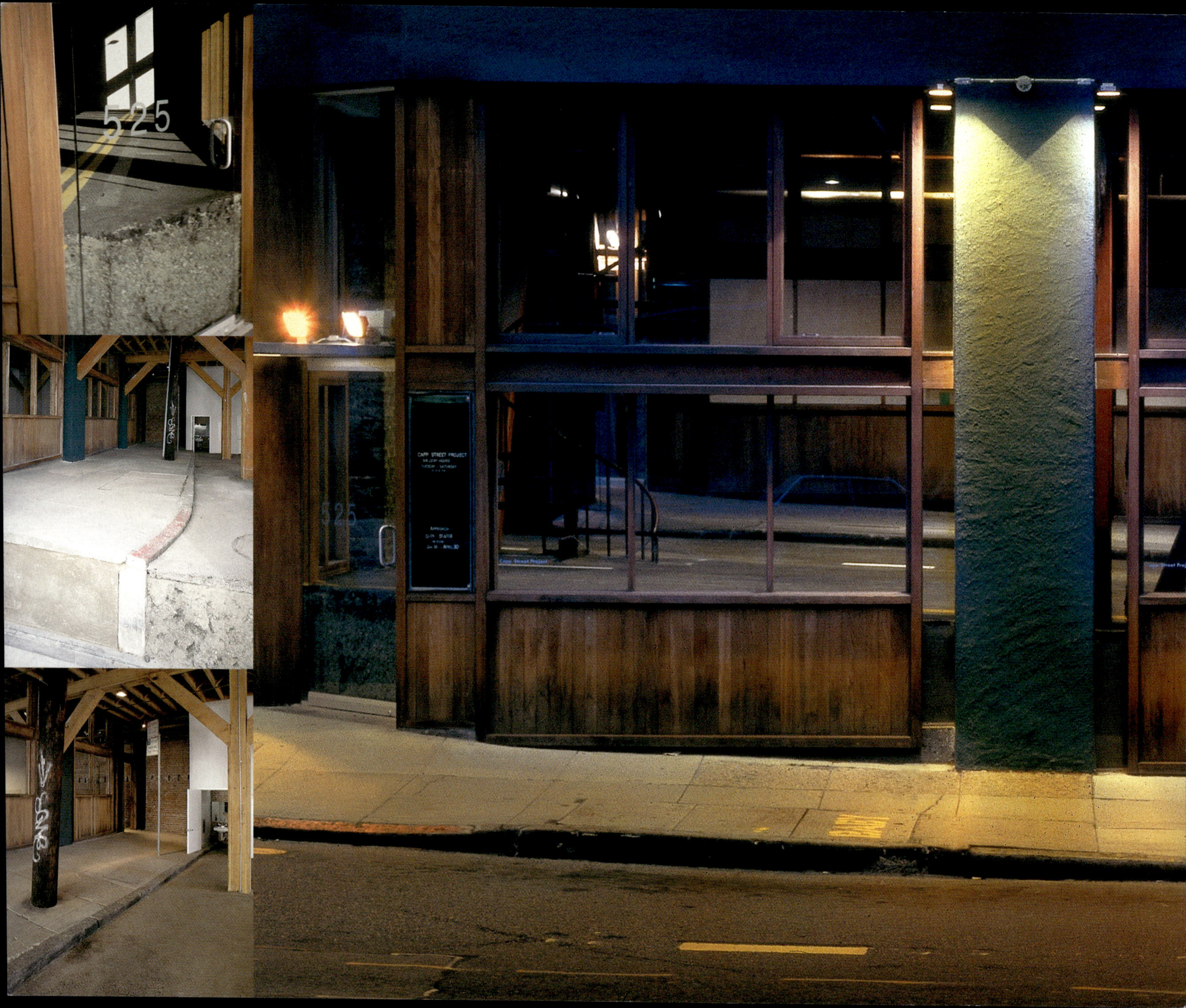
525
CAPP STREET PROJECT
GALLERY HOURS
TUESDAY - SATURDAY
APPROACH
GARY SIMMONS
JAN 30 - APRIL 30

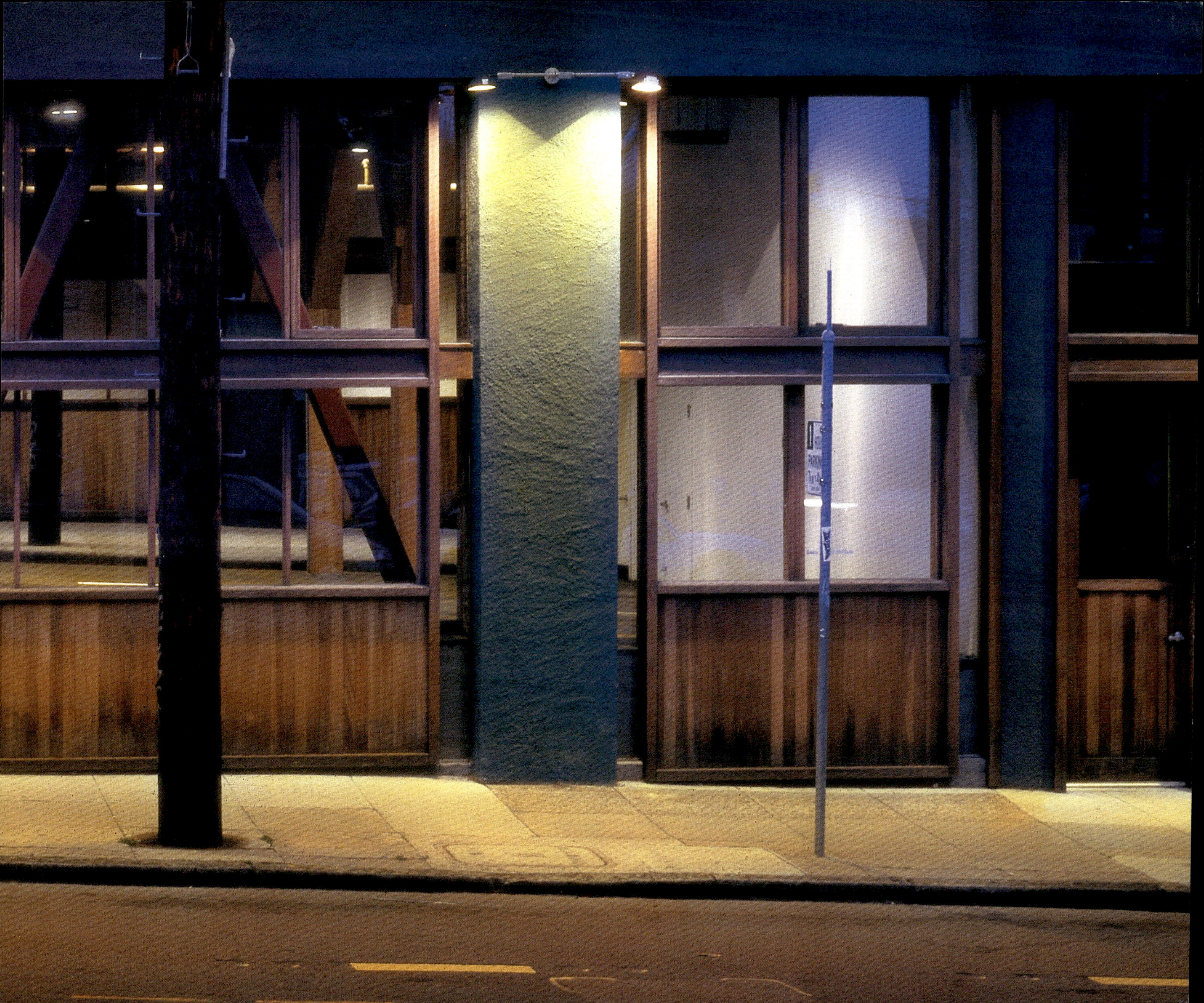

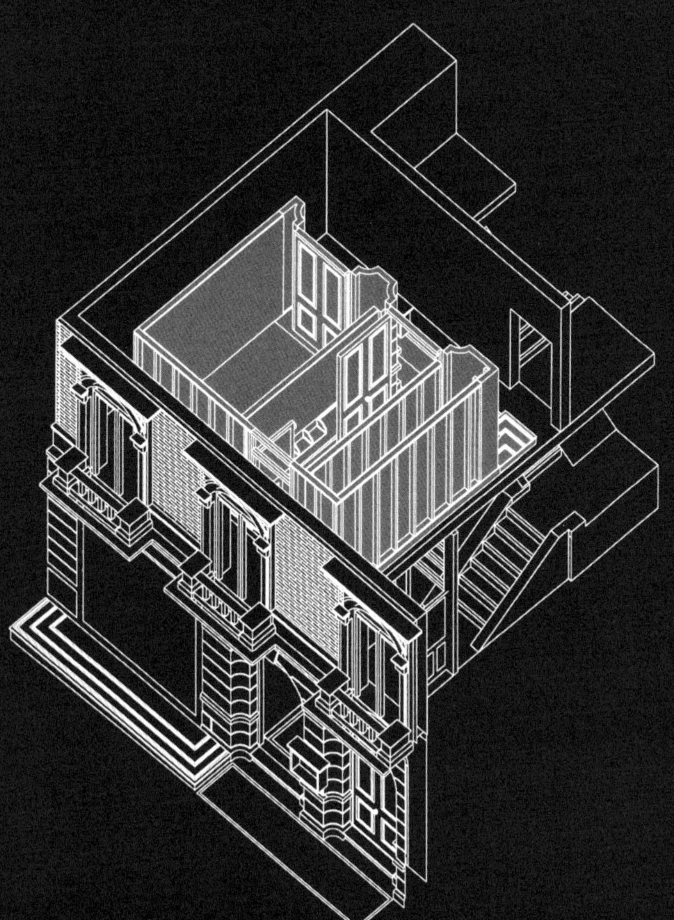

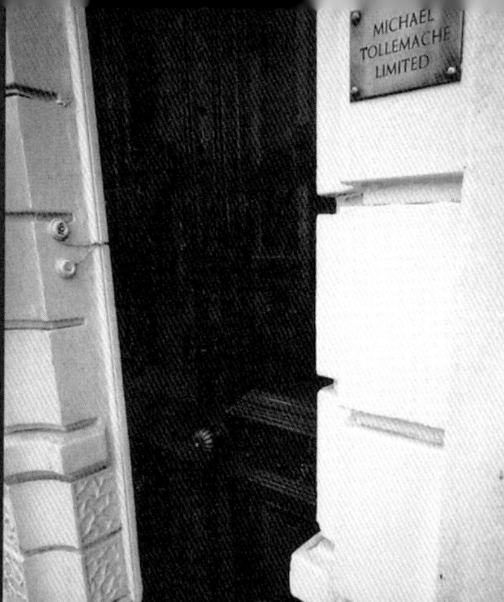

within the line of the studs

1997

wood, gypsum, sheetrock, terrazzo, marble, glass, metals, linoleum, electrical fittings, coconut matting, paint

9' x 12' x 13'

Jay Jopling/White Cube, London

The full-scale reconstruction of the building's "forecourt", façade and entrance hall is presented as a sculpture, raised and separated from the architecture of the gallery. The visitor enters the building from the street through the green door into a small corridor and proceeds up two flights of stairs to the White Cube gallery space. Upon entering, one is once again confronted with the building's façade. Two corridors are formed: one replicated, the other created by the close proximity of the exterior of the piece to the existing gallery walls. The second green door – that of the neighboring coin shop – is locked.

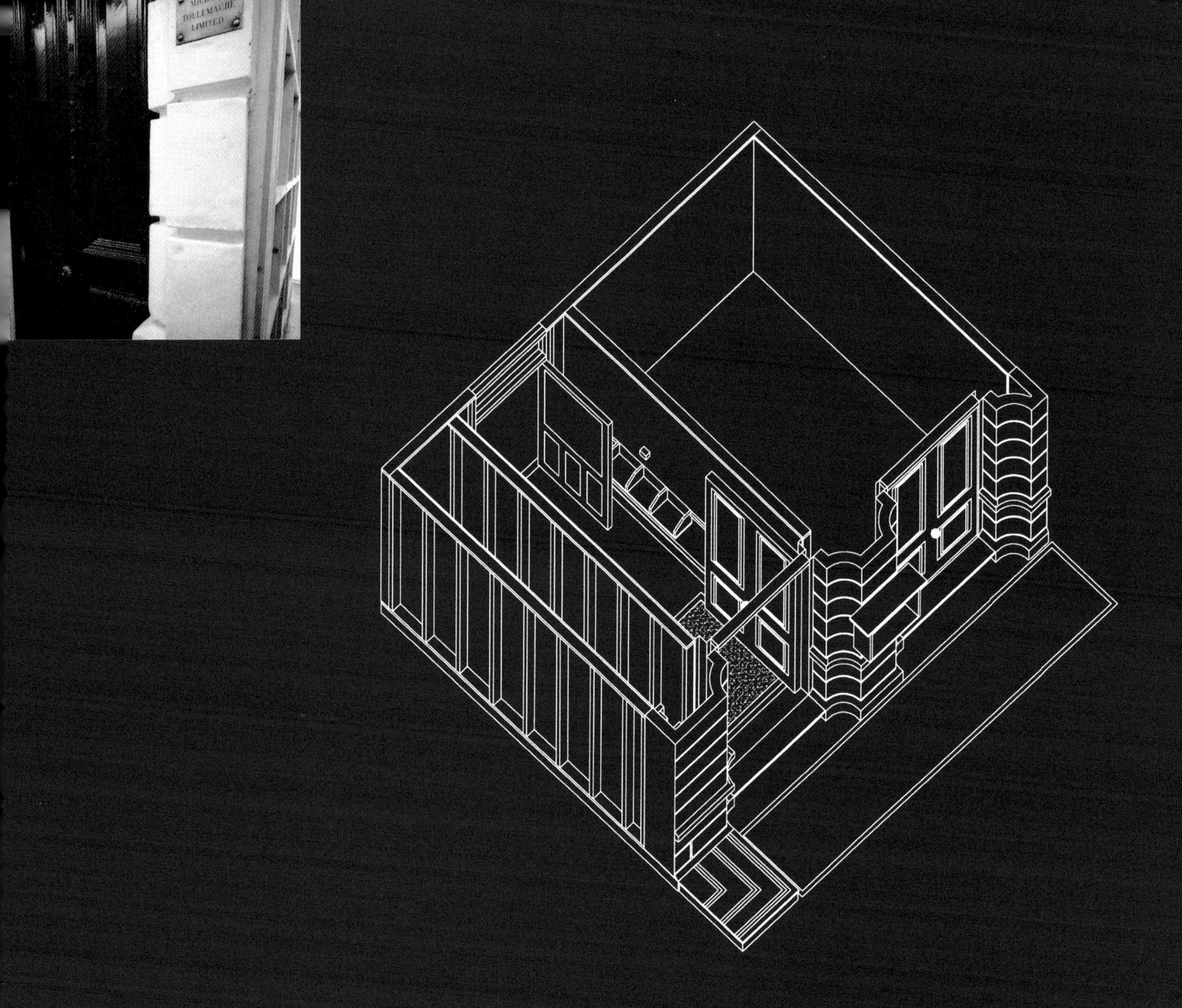
TOLLEMACHE
LIMITED

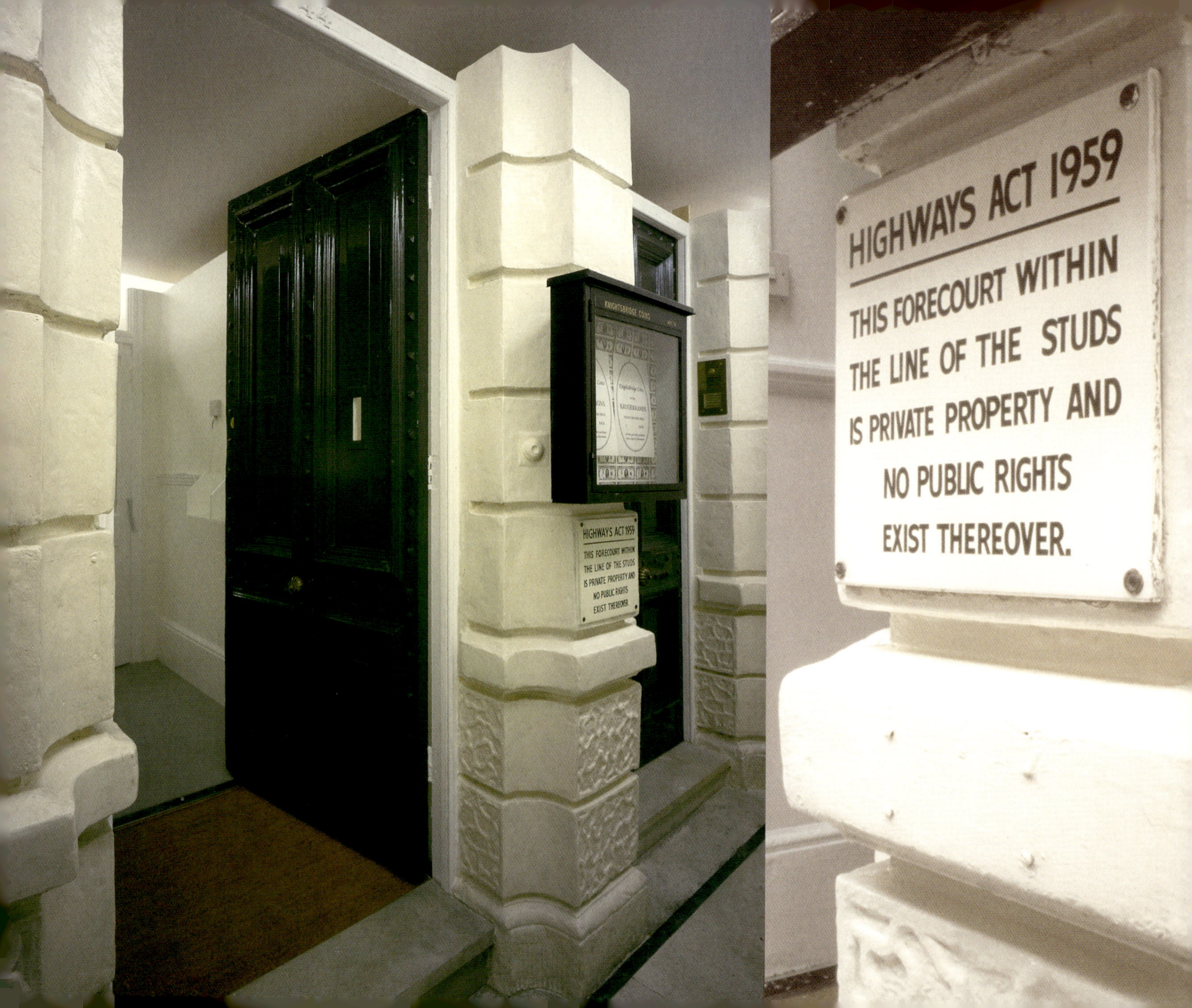
HIGHWAYS ACT 1959
THIS FORECOURT WITHIN
THE LINE OF THE STUDS
IS PRIVATE PROPERTY AND
NO PUBLIC RIGHTS
EXIST THEREOVER.
KNIGHTSBRIDGE COINS
HIGHWAYS ACT 1959
THIS FORECOURT WITHIN
THE LINE OF THE STUDS
IS PRIVATE PROPERTY AND
NO PUBLIC RIGHTS
EXIST THEREOVER.

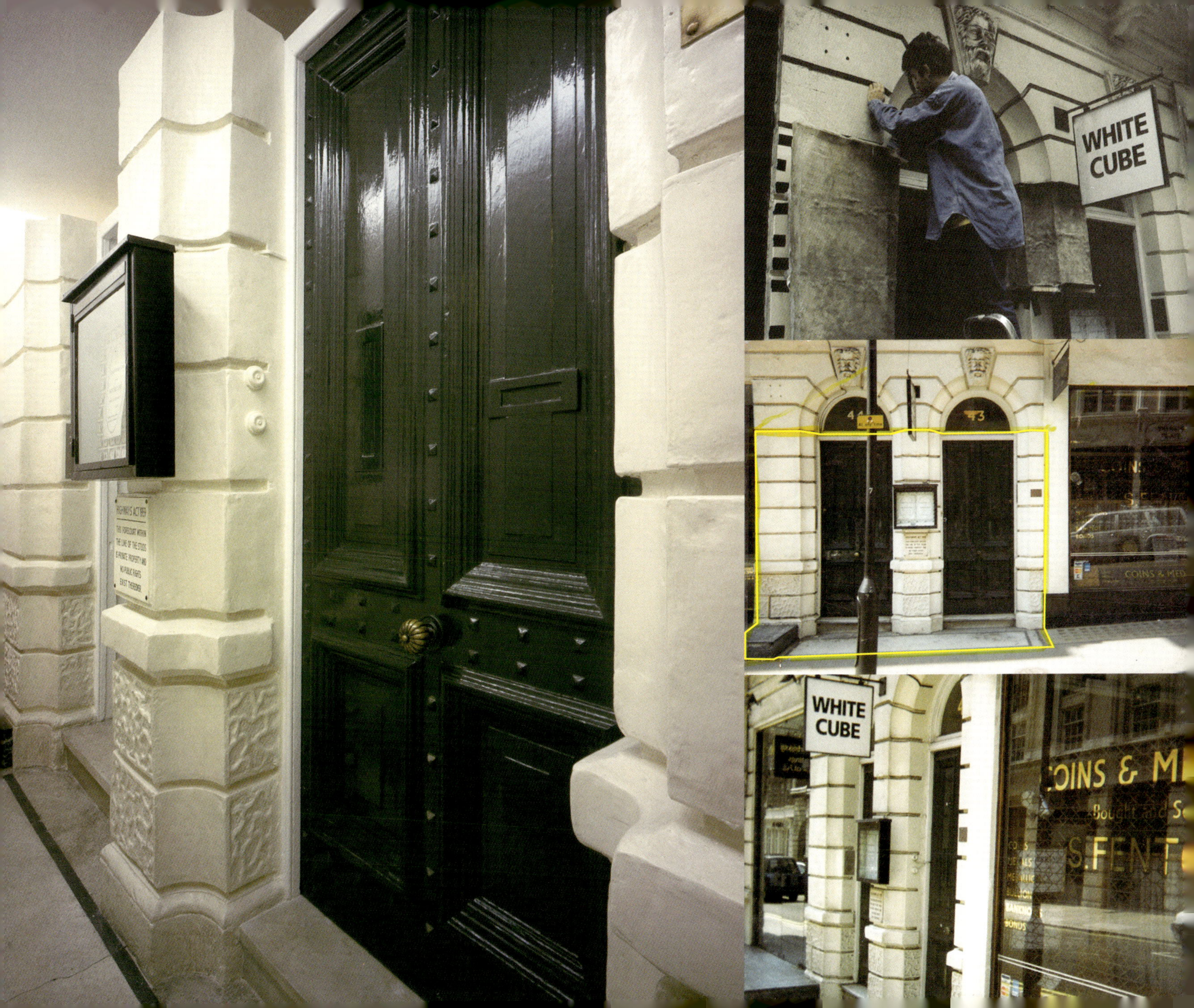

WHITE CUBE
WHITE CUBE
COINS & M
S. FENT

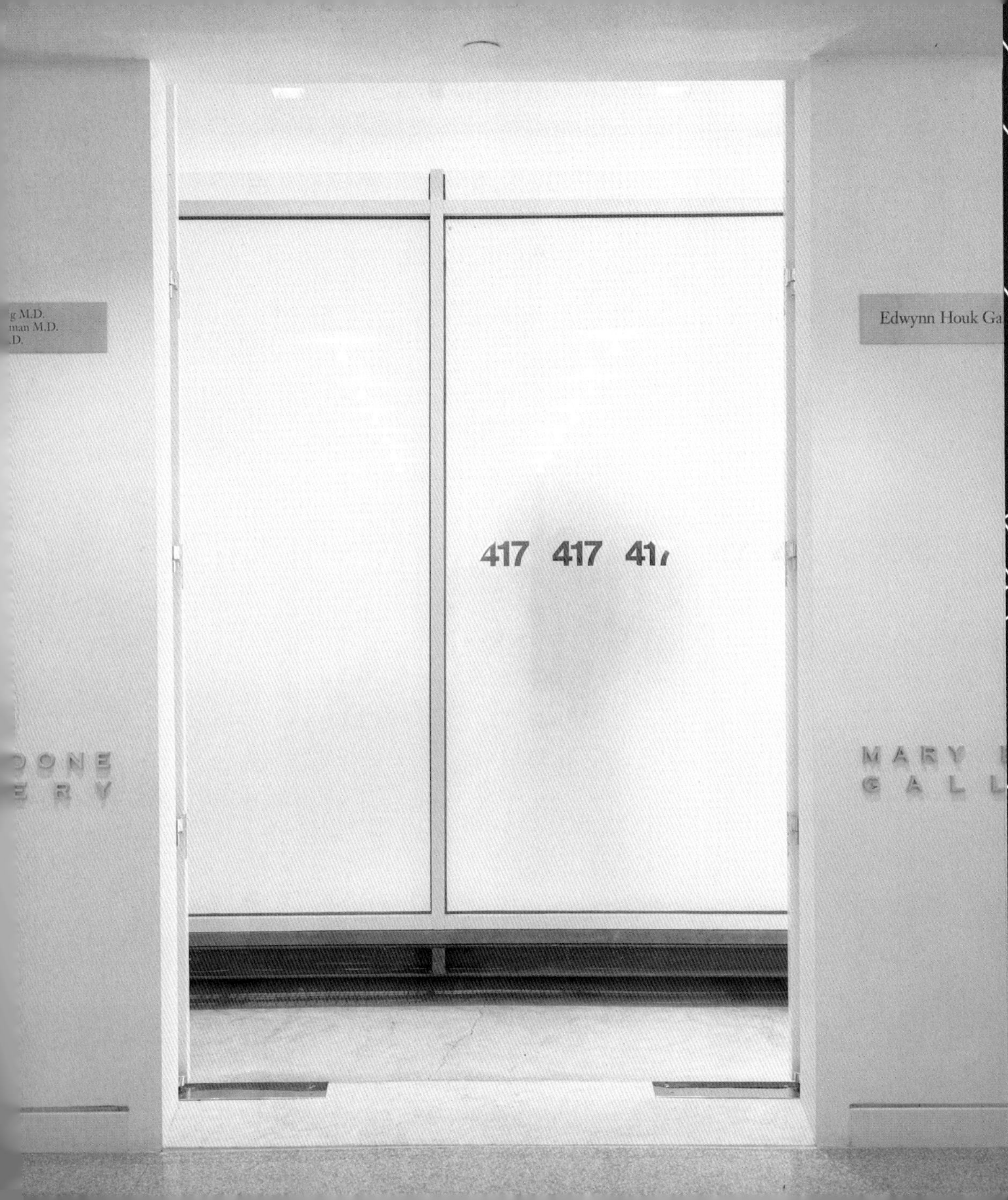

417 417 41

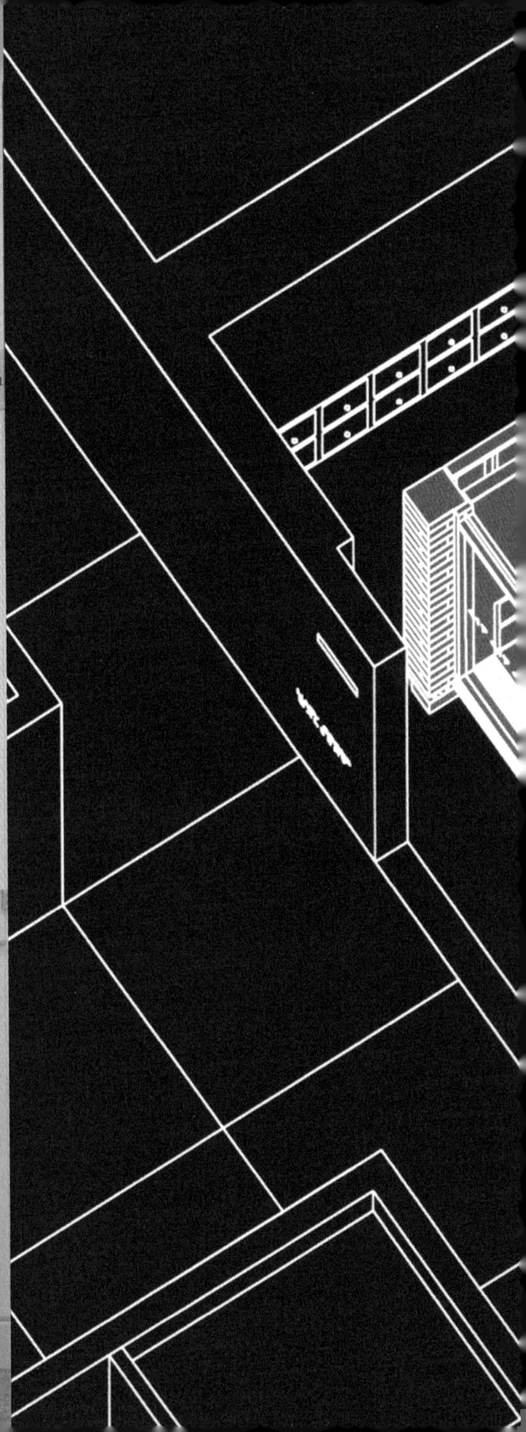

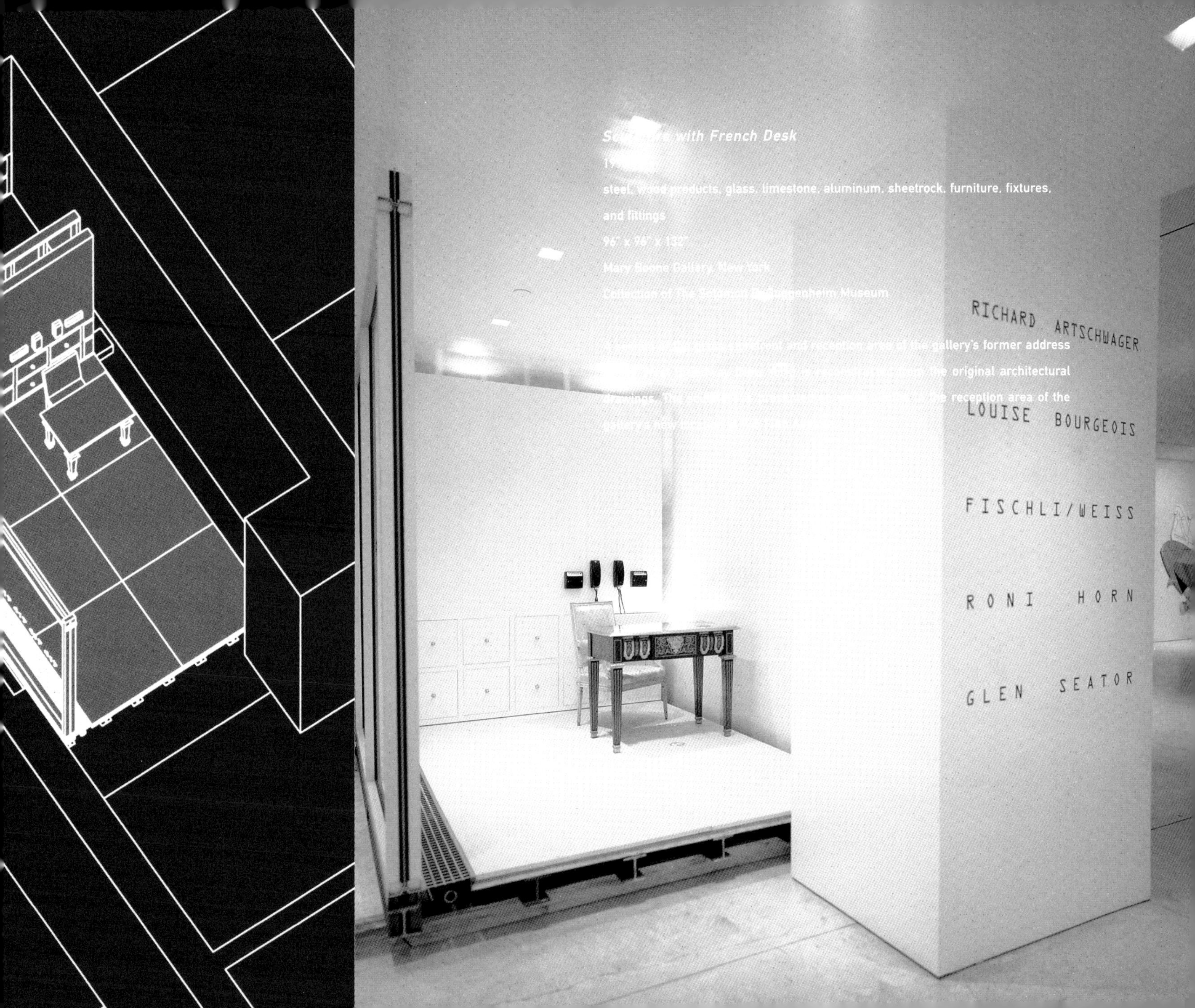

Sculpture with French Desk
19
steel, wood products, glass, limestone, aluminum, sheetrock, furniture, fixtures,
and fittings
96" x 96" x 132"
Mary Boone Gallery, New York
Collection of The Solomon R. Guggenheim Museum
and reception area of the gallery's former address
the original architectural
the reception area of the
RICHARD ARTSCHWAGER
LOUISE BOURGEOIS
FISCHLI/WEISS
RONI HORN
GLEN SEATOR

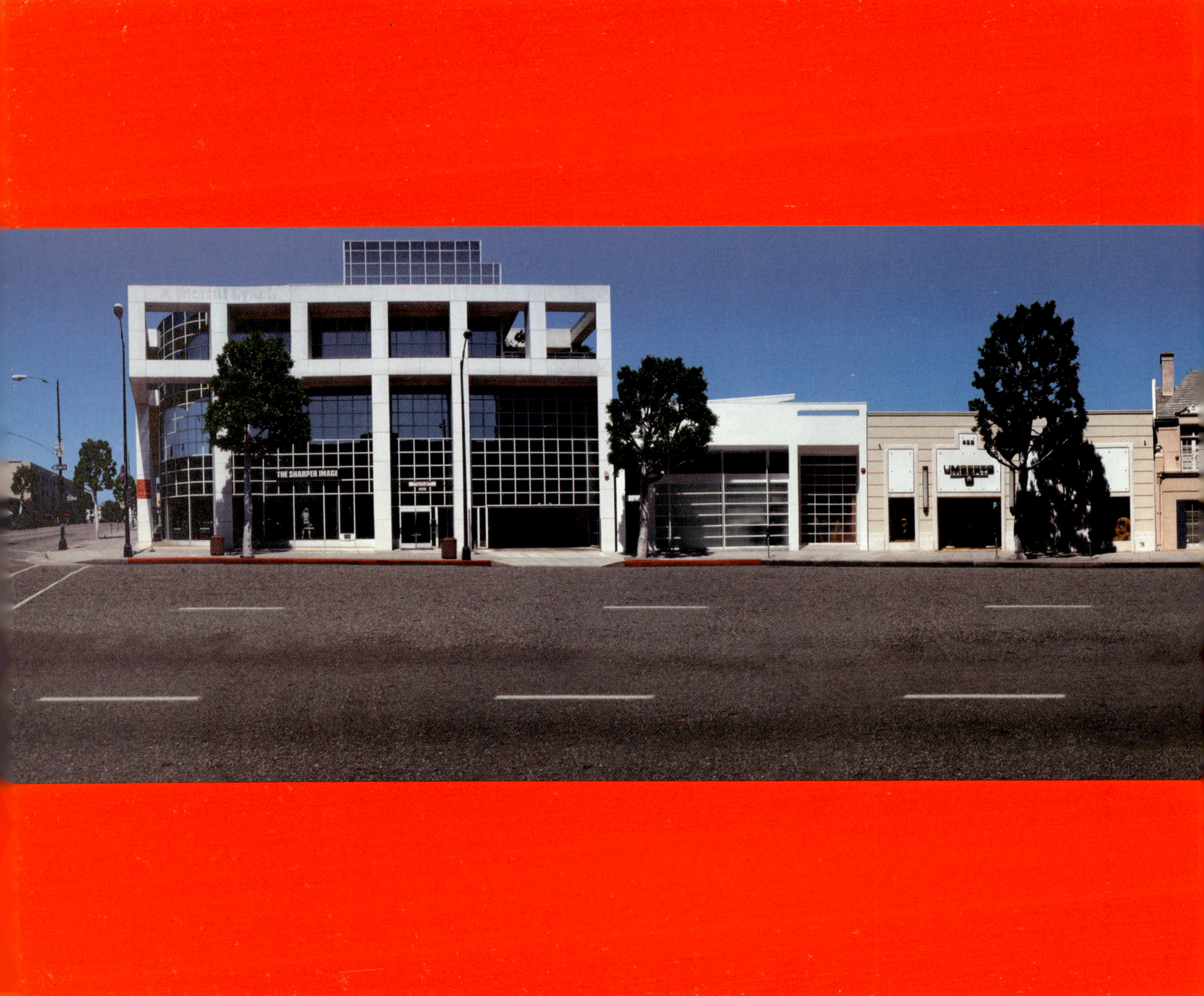

THE SHARPER IMAGE